THE UNITED STATES
AND
CENTRAL AMERICA

THE UNITED STATES
AND
CENTRAL AMERICA

GEOPOLITICAL REALITIES
AND REGIONAL FRAGILITY

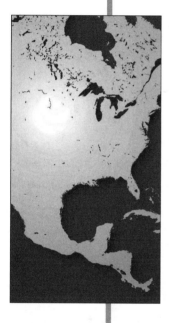

Mark B. Rosenberg
and
Luis G. Solís

ROUTLEDGE
New York • London

Routledge
Taylor & Francis Group
270 Madison Avenue
New York, NY 10016

Routledge
Taylor & Francis Group
2 Park Square
Milton Park, Abingdon
Oxon OX14 4RN

© 2007 by Taylor & Francis Group, LLC
Routledge is an imprint of Taylor & Francis Group, an Informa business

Printed in the United States of America on acid-free paper
10 9 8 7 6 5 4 3 2 1

International Standard Book Number-10: 0-415-95835-0 (Softcover) 0-415-95834-2 (Hardcover)
International Standard Book Number-13: 978-0-415-95835-6 (Softcover) 978-0-415-95834-9 (Hardcover)

Library of Congress Cataloging-in-Publication Data

Rosenberg, Mark, 1949-
   United States and Central America : geopolitical realities and regional fragility /
Mark B. Rosenberg, Luis G. Solís.
      p. cm. -- (Contemporary inter-American relations series)
      Includes bibliographical references.
      ISBN 978-0-415-95834-9 (alk. paper) -- ISBN 978-0-415-95835-6 (alk. paper)
      1. Central America--Foreign relations--United States. 2. United States--Foreign
relations--Central America. 3. United States--Foreign relations--1989- 4. Geopolitics.
I. Solís Rivera, Luis Guillermo. II. Title.

   F1436.8.U6R67 2007
   327.730728--dc22   2006102720

Visit the Taylor & Francis Web site at
http://www.taylorandfrancis.com

and the Routledge Web site at
http://www.routledge.com

Contents

Preface

The transition from authoritarian rule to constitutional government
The continent-wide economic depression of the 1980s and the
  subsequent shift toward more open market-conforming economies
The end of the Cold War in Europe
The transformation of relations with the United States

Each of these major events and processes was an epochal change in the history of Latin America and the Caribbean. More striking is that all four changes took place within the same relatively short time, though not all four affected every country in the same way. They became interconnected, with change on each dimension fostering convergent changes on other dimensions. Thus, by the beginning of the new millennium, we had witnessed an important transformation and intensification in U.S.–Latin American relations.

This book is part of a series of ten books on U.S. relations with Latin American and Caribbean countries. Each of these books is focused on the fourth of these four transformations—namely, the change in U.S. relations with Latin America and the Caribbean. Our premise is that the first three transformations provide pieces of the explanation for the change in U.S. relations with its neighbors in the Americas and for the changes in the foreign policies of Latin American and Caribbean states. Each of the books in the series assesses the impact of the epoch-making changes upon each other.

The process of widest impact was the economic transformation. By the end of 1982, much of North America, Western Europe, and East Asia launched into an economic boom at the very time when Latin America plunged into an economic depression of great severity that lasted approximately to the end of the decade. As a consequence of such economic collapse, nearly all Latin American governments readjusted their economic strategies. They departed from principal reliance on import-substitution industrialization, opened their economies to international trade and investment, and adopted policies to create more open market-conforming economies. (Even Cuba had changed its economic strategy by the 1990s, making its economy more open to foreign direct investment and trade.)

The region-wide economic changes had direct and immediate impact upon U.S.–Latin American relations. The share of U.S. trade accounted for by Latin America and the Caribbean had declined fairly steadily from the end of World War II to the end of the 1980s. In the 1990s, in contrast, U.S. trade with Latin America grew at a rate significantly faster than the growth of U.S. trade worldwide; Latin America had become the fastest growing market for U.S. exports. The United States, at long last, did take notice of Latin America. Trade between some Latin American countries also boomed, especially within subregions such as the southern cone of South America, Venezuela and Colombia, the Central American countries, and, to a lesser extent, the anglophone Caribbean countries. The establishment of formal freer-trade areas facilitated the growth of trade and other economic relations. These included the North American Free Trade Agreement (NAFTA), which grouped Mexico, the United States, and Canada; the MERCOSUR (Common Market of the South), with Argentina, Brazil, Paraguay, and Uruguay; the Andean Community, whose members were Bolivia, Colombia, Ecuador, Peru, and Venezuela; the Central American Common Market (CACM); and the Caribbean Community (CARICOM). U.S. direct and portfolio investment in large quantities flowed into Latin America and the Caribbean, financing the expansion of tradable economic activities. The speed of portfolio investment transactions, however, also exposed these and other countries to marked financial volatility and recurrent financial panics. The transformation in hemispheric international economic relations—specifically in U.S. economic relations with the rest of the hemisphere—was already far-reaching as the twenty-first century began.

These structural economic changes had specific and common impacts on the conduct of international economic diplomacy. All governments in the Americas, large and small, had to develop a cadre of experts who could negotiate concrete, technical trade, investment, and other economic issues with the United States and with other countries in the region. All had to create teams of international trade lawyers and experts capable of defending national interests and the interests of particular business firms, in international, inter-American, or subregional dispute-resolution panels or court-like proceedings. The discourse and practice of inter-American relations, broadly understood, became much more professional—less the province of eloquent poets and more the domain of number-crunching litigators and mediators.

The changes in Latin America's domestic political regimes began in the late 1970s. These, too, would contribute to change the texture of inter-American relations. By the end of the 1990s, democratization based on fair elections, competitive parties, constitutionalism, and respect for the rule of law and the liberties of citizens had advanced and was still advancing throughout the region, albeit unevenly and with persisting serious problems, Cuba being the principal exception. In 2000, for example, for the first time since their revolution, Mexicans elected an opposition candidate, Vicente Fox, to the presidency, and Alberto Fujimori was compelled to resign in Peru, accused of abuse of power, electoral fraud, and corruption. In each instance, the cause of democratization advanced.

Democratization also affected the international relations of Latin American and Caribbean countries, albeit in more subtle ways. The anglophone Caribbean is a largely archipelagic region, long marked by the widespread practice of constitutional government. Since the 1970s, anglophone Caribbean democratic governments rallied repeatedly to defend constitutional government on any of the islands where it came under threat and, in the specific cases of Grenada and Guyana, to assist the process of democratization in the 1980s and 1990s, respectively. In the 1990s, Latin American governments also began to act collectively to defend and promote democratic rule; with varying degrees of success and U.S. support, they did so in Guatemala, Haiti, Paraguay, and Peru. Democratization had a more complex relationship to the content of specific foreign policies. In the 1990s, democratization in Argentina, Brazil, Uruguay, and Chile contributed to improved international political, security, and economic relations among these southern cone countries. Yet, at times, democratic politics made it more difficult to manage international relations over boundary or territorial issues between given pairs of countries, including Colombia and Venezuela and Costa Rica and Nicaragua. In general, democratization facilitated better relations between Latin American and Caribbean countries, on the one hand, and the United States, on the other. Across the Americas, democratic governments, including the United States and Canada, acted to defend and promote constitutional government. Much cooperation over security, including the attempt to foster cooperative security and civilian supremacy over the military, would have been unthinkable except in the new, deeper democratic context in the hemisphere.

At its best, in the 1990s, democratic politics made it possible to transform the foreign policies of particular presidential administrations into the foreign policies of states. For example, Argentina's principal political parties endorsed the broad outlines of their nation's foreign policy, including the framework to govern much friendlier Argentinean relations with the United States. All Chilean political parties were strongly committed to their country's transformation into an international trading state. The principal political parties of the anglophone Caribbean sustained consistent long-lasting foreign policies across different partisan administrations. Mexico's three leading political parties agreed, even if they differed on specifics, that NAFTA should be implemented, binding Mexico to the United States and Canada. Also, the George H. W. Bush and William Clinton administrations in the United States followed remarkably compatible policies toward Latin America and the Caribbean with regard to the promotion of free trade, pacification in Central America, support for international financial institutions, and the defense of constitutional government in Latin America and the Caribbean. Both administrations acted in concert with other states in the region and often through the Organization of American States. Democratic procedures, in these and other cases, establish the credibility of a state's foreign policy, because all actors would have reason to expect that the framework of today's foreign policy would endure tomorrow.

The end of the Cold War in Europe began following the accession in 1985 of Mikhail Gorbachev to the post of general-secretary of the Communist Party of the Soviet Union. The end accelerated during the second half of the 1980s, culminating with the collapse of communist regimes in Europe between 1989 and 1991 and the breakup of the Soviet Union in late 1991. The impact of the end of the U.S.–Soviet conflict on the hemisphere was subtle but important: the United States was no longer obsessed with the threat of communism. Freed to focus on other international interests, the United States discovered that it shared many practical interests with Latin American and Caribbean countries; the latter, in turn, found it easier to cooperate with the United States. There was one exception to this benign international process. The United States was also freed to forget its long-lasting fear of Communist guerrillas in Colombia (which remained powerful and continued to operate nonetheless) in order to concentrate on a "war" against drug trafficking, even if it undermined Colombia's constitutional regime.

The process of ending the Cold War also had a specific component in the Western Hemisphere, namely, the termination of the civil and international wars that had swirled in Central America since the late 1970s. The causes of those wars had been internal and international. In the early

1990s the collapse of the Soviet Union and the marked weakening of Cuban influence enabled the U.S. government to support negotiations with governments or insurgent movements it had long opposed. All of these international changes made it easier to arrange for domestic political, military, and social settlements of the wars in and around Nicaragua, El Salvador, and Guatemala. The end of the Cold War in Europe had an extraordinary impact on Cuba as well. The Cold War did not end the sharp conflict between the U.S. and Cuban governments, but the latter was deprived of Soviet support, forcing it to recall its troops overseas, open its economy to the world, and lower its foreign policy profile. The United States felt freer to conduct a "Colder War" against Cuba, seeking to overthrow its government.

Two other large-scale processes, connected to the previous three, had a significant impact in the international relations of the Western Hemisphere. They were the booms in international migration and cocaine-related international organized crime. Migration and organized crime on an international scale in the Americas are as old as the European settlement begun in the late fifteenth century and the growth of state-sponsored piracy in the sixteenth century, yet the volume and acceleration of these two processes in the 1980s and 1990s were truly extraordinary.

Widespread violence in Central America and Colombia and economic depression everywhere accelerated the rate of emigration to the United States. Once begun, the process of migration to the United States was sustained through networks of relatives and friends, the family-unification provisions of U.S. legislation, and the relatively lower costs of international transportation and communication. By the mid-1990s, over 12 million people born in Latin America resided in the United States; two-thirds of them had arrived since 1980. The number of people of Latin American ancestry in the United States was even larger, of course. In the 1980s, migrants came to the United States not just from countries such as Mexico of traditional emigration, but also from countries such as Brazil that in the past had generated few emigrants. As the twentieth century ended, the United States had become one of the largest "Latin American" countries in the Americas. The United States had also come to play a major role in the production and consumption of the culture, including music, book publishing, and television programming, of the Spanish-speaking peoples. All of these trends are likely to intensify in the twenty-first century.

Had this series of books been published in the mid-1970s, coca and cocaine would have merited brief mention in one or two of the books, and no mention in most of them. The boom in U.S. cocaine consumption in the late 1970s and 1980s changed this. The region-wide economic collapse of the 1980s made it easier to bribe public officials, judges, police, and military officers. U.S. cocaine supply interdiction policies in the 1980s raised the price of cocaine, making the coca and cocaine businesses the most lucrative in depression-ravaged economies. The generally unregulated sale of weapons in the United States equipped gangsters throughout the Americas. Bolivia and Peru produced the coca. Colombians grew it, refined it, and financed it. Criminal gangs in the Caribbean, Central America, and Mexico transported and distributed it. Everywhere, drug traffic-related violence and corruption escalated.

The impact of economic policy change, democratization, and the end of the Cold War in Europe on U.S.–Latin American relations, therefore, provides important explanations common to the countries of the Americas in their relations with the United States. The acceleration of emigration and the construction and development of international organized crime around the cocaine business were also key common themes in the continent's international relations during the closing fifth of the twentieth century. To the extent that they are pertinent, these topics appear in each of the books in this series. Nonetheless, each country's own history, geographic location, set of neighbors, resource endowment, institutional features, and leadership characteristics bear as well on the construction, design, and implementation of its foreign policy. These more particular factors enrich and guide the books in this series in their interplay with the more general arguments.

At the end of the 1990s and in the early twenty-first century, dark clouds reappeared on the firmament of inter-American relations, raising doubts about the optimistic trajectory that seemed set at the beginning of the 1990s. The heavy influence of the military on civilian society was significantly felt in Colombia, Venezuela, and Peru (until the end of Alberto Fujimori's presidency in November 2000). In January 2000, a military coup overthrew the constitutionally elected president of Ecuador, although the civilian vice-president soon reestablished constitutional government. Serious concerns resurfaced concerning the depth and durability of democratic institutions and practices in these countries. Venezuela seemed ready to try once again much greater government involvement in economic affairs. The president and assembly were stalemated in Nicaragua.

Argentina's spectacular economic crisis in 2002 grievously injured its people; the nation's prospects for a quick economic recovery (akin to the quick recoveries from financial crises in Mexico after 1995 and Brazil in 1999) were poor. The Argentine economic crisis, in turn, generated severe economic pressures, especially on Uruguay and Paraguay and, to a lesser extent, on Brazil. The United States responded slowly and ineptly to the evolving economic crisis in the southern cone, although in August 2002 at long last it joined an international coalition to provide significant financial support to Brazil and Uruguay. Also, the United States had held back from implementing the commitment to hemispheric free trade that both presidents George H. W. Bush and William Clinton had pledged. These trends could adversely affect the future of a Western Hemisphere based on free politics, free markets, and peace. Nevertheless, in 2005, the U.S. Congress ratified the U.S. free trade agreement with Central American countries and the Dominican Republic, the so-called Central American Free Trade Agreement (CAFTA), reopening the chapter of freer trade in the Americas.

This Project

Each of the books in this series has two authors, typically one from a Latin American or Caribbean country (or, in the case of this book, a subregion) and another from the United States. We chose this approach to facilitate the writing of the books and ensure that the books would represent a broad international perspective. In addition, we sought to embed each book within international networks of scholarly work in more than one country.

We have attempted to write short books that ask common questions to enable various readers—scholars, students, public officials, international entrepreneurs, and the educated public—to make their own comparisons and judgments as they read two or more volumes in the series. The project sought to foster comparability across the books through two conferences held at the Instituto Tecnológico Autónomo de México (ITAM) in Mexico City. The first, held in June 1998, compared ideas and questions; the second, held in August 1999, discussed preliminary drafts of the books. Both of us read and commented on all the manuscripts; the manuscripts also received commentary from other authors in the project. We hope that the network of scholars created for this project will continue to function, even if informally, and that the Web page created for this project will provide access for a wider audience to the ideas, research, and writing associated with it.

We are grateful to the Ford Foundation for its principal support of this project and to Cristina Eguizábal for her advice and assistance throughout this endeavor. We are also grateful to the MacArthur Foundation for the support that made it possible to hold a second successful project conference in Mexico City. The Rockefeller Foundation provided the two of us with an opportunity to spend four splendid weeks in Bellagio, Italy, working on our various general responsibilities in this project. The Academic Department of International Studies at ITAM hosted the project throughout its duration and the two international conferences. We appreciate the support of the Asociación Mexicana de Cultura, ITAM's principal supporter in this work. Harvard University's Weatherhead Center for International Affairs also supported aspects of this project, as did Harvard University's David Rockefeller Center for Latin American Studies. We are particularly grateful to Hazel Blackmore and Juana Gómez at ITAM and Amanda Pearson and Kathleen Hoover at the Weatherhead Center for their work on many aspects of the project. At Routledge, Melissa Rosati encouraged us from the start; Eric Nelson supported the project through its conclusion; and Robert Tempio has guided the project through its continuing implementation.

Jorge I. Domínguez
Rafael Fernández de Castro
Harvard University ITAM

Acknowledgments

We both want to acknowledge the patience, support, and confidence from the series editors Jorge Domínguez and Rafael Fernández de Castro. Their thoughtfulness in developing this series and their careful guidance were invaluable to our entire team.

We have had the unflagging support of our families and want to express our deep appreciation for their understanding during our six-year odyssey to put this book together. We are particularly grateful to Rosalie, Ben, and Ginelle Rosenberg and to all the Solis–Worsfold and Solis–Penas families in Costa Rica for their unending support and affection. We are indebted to colleagues Cresencio Arcos, Cristina Eguizabal, Eduardo Gamarra, Douglas Kincaid, Modesto Maidique, Anthony Maingot, James Mau, Francisco Rojas, and John Stack for their thoughtful support and encouragement for our work.

This book would not have been possible without the support of our determined graduate and undergraduate students at Florida International University, FUNPADEM, and the Universidad de Costa Rica, including Kelly Kirchner, Annette Rasco, Robert Ortiz, Jonathan Cameron, Luis Perez, Carlos Manrara, and Daniel Matul, Jennifer Charpentier, and Stella Sáenz.

We are indebted to Eloísa Echazábal and Mercedes Rodríguez in the Office of Academic Affairs at Florida International University. Their assistance in keeping us moving proved instrumental during the final months of writing this book. In particular, Mercedes used her talents to supervise the research, assemble and edit the manuscript, craft the tables and maps, and coordinate its many details up to publication.

We of course bear the final responsibility for any errors and omissions that the reader may encounter and encourage you to communicate directly with us any concerns, doubts, comments, and criticisms that may improve the interpretations we offer in this book.

Mark B. Rosenberg
Miami and Tallahassee, Florida

Luis Guillermo Solís
San José, Costa Rica

Acronyms

AFL–CIO	American Federation of Labor–Congress of Industrial Organizations
AID	Agency for International Development
ALIDES	Central American Alliance for Sustainable Development
CAFTA	Central America Free Trade Agreement
CAFTA-DR	Central America and the Dominican Republic Free Trade Agreement
CARICOM	Caribbean Community
CBI	Caribbean Basin Initiative
CFAC	Armed Forces Conference on Central America
CIA	Central Intelligence Agency
CIE	Bureau of Customs and Immigration Enforcement
CONCA–USA	Joint Declaration Central America–the United States of America
DEA	Drug Enforcement Administration
FECON	Federation of Environmental Conservation
FMF	Foreign Military Financing
FMLN	Farabundo Martí National Liberation Front
FSLN	Sandinista National Liberation Front
FTAA	Free Trade Area of the Americas
GATT	General Agreement on Tariffs and Trade

GDP	Gross Domestic Product
IESC	International Executive Service Corps
ILO	International Labor Organization
LULAC	League of United Latin American Citizens
MCA	Millennium Challenge Account
MERCOSUR	Common Market of the South
MS	Mara Salvatrucha
NAFTA	North American Free Trade Agreement
NATO	North Atlantic Treaty Organization
NGO	Nongovernmental organization
OAS	Organization of American States
PROARCA	Regional Environmental Program for Central America
SEATO	South East Asia Treaty Organization
SICA	Central American Integration System
SOUTHCOM	United States Southern Command
TIAR	Inter-American Treaty of Reciprocal Assistance
TPS	Temporary Protection Status
UN	United Nations
UNCED	United Nations Conference on the Environment and Development
UNO	National Opposition Union
US	United States
USAID	United States Agency for International Development
USSR	United Soviet Socialist Republic
USTR	United States Trade Representative
WTO	World Trade Organization

Introduction: Central America and the United States in the Post–Cold War

Premises and challenges

For Central America, as for the rest of the world, the post–Cold War era's uncertainty and unpredictability in global affairs constituted an unprecedented opportunity to break out of its subordinate relationship with the United States. This was a relationship that had been cemented in part through the shared concern for Soviet penetration and anticommunism for almost half a century. The absence of a "reliable road map for this constantly changing international landscape"[1] following the collapse of the Soviet Union made it difficult to assess the prospects for U.S.–Central American affairs during this period. Clearly, however, the shrinking presence of the United States following a decade of intense engagement during the 1980s provided Central America with a new opportunity for greater autonomy from U.S. foreign policy.

This opportunity was stillborn with the deadly terrorist attacks on New York and Washington on September 11, 2001 (9-11). Consequently, two considerations are taken into account to understand the dynamics of U.S.–Central American affairs since this milestone in global affairs. First, the terrorist attack brought post–Cold War U.S. security policy into focus in the same manner as the threat of Soviet communism galvanized five decades of U.S. foreign policy during the Cold War. Just as President Harry Truman (1945–1953) took the first significant U.S. initiative in 1947 by

1

Table 1 The Truman Doctrine and the Bush National Security Strategy

	Truman[a]	Bush[b]
Premise	I believe that it must be the policy of the United States to support free people that are resisting attempted subjugation by armed minorities or by outside pressures.	Defending our Nation against its enemies is the first and fundamental commitment of the Federal government. Today that task has changed dramatically. The United States is fighting a war against terrorists of global reach.
Threat	The seeds of totalitarian regimes are nurtured by misery and want. They spread and grow in the evil soil of poverty and strife. They reach their full growth when the hope of a people for a better life has died. We must keep that hope alive. If we falter in our leadership, we may endanger the peace of the world—and we shall surely endanger the welfare of our own nation.	Enemies in the past needed great armies to endanger America. Now shadowy networks of individuals can bring great chaos and suffering to our shores for less than it costs to purchase a single tank. Terrorists are organized to penetrate open societies, and to turn the power of modern technologies against us.

[a] *President Harry S. Truman's address before a Joint Session of Congress,* March 12, 1947. *The Avalon Project at Yale Law School,* http://www.yale.edu/lawweb/avalon/trudoc.htm.

[b] The White House, *The National Security Strategy of the United States of America,* September 2002.

enunciating his "doctrine" that pledged to provide American economic and military assistance to any nation threatened by communism,[2] President George W. Bush's September 2002 "National Security Strategy of the United States" now informs the highest domain of U.S. foreign policy decision-making. It focuses on the country's national security defined in terms of defending it against its enemies. According to President Bush, the "gravest danger our Nation faces lies at the crossroads of radicalism and technology," in the hands of a hostile nation or a single-minded terrorist. Table 1 summarizes these two policy statements.

A second consideration relates to the blurring of distinctions between domestic and international politics. *Intermestic* issues have emerged as key to understanding U.S. policy toward the region. Intermestic issues combine foreign and domestic policy issues and actors in new ways. They reflect the commonly repeated adage in the United States that "all politics are local," particularly in the post–Cold War era. The emergence of the intermestic phenomenon also reflects the reality that U.S. foreign policy, outside of critical national security issues defined by Cold War anticommunism and post–Cold War antiterrorism, is born from (or else is profoundly conditioned by) conflicts that spring from, among other factors, regional, uneven growth, and development within the United States.[3]

The ascent of regionalism in U.S. foreign policy explains the mobilization of single-issue interest groups and coalitions of interests, both domestic and foreign, that continuously lobby Congress and the White House.[4] It also highlights the ascent of private, nongovernmental actors (the so-called

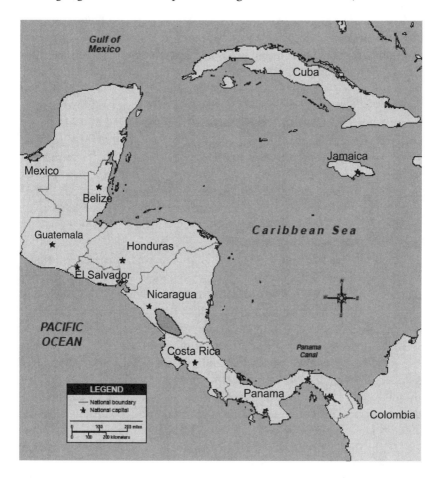

Figure 1 Map of the Central American republics.

civil society) in a turf traditionally monopolized by diplomats and other state and federal officials. It is true that the formal authority and roles of the Congress and the Executive Branch as the sole bearers of national representation continues to dominate foreign policy-making. Yet, at the threshold of the twenty-first century, it would be impossible to deny the significant advances and growing influence that business, environmental, humanitarian, labor, and academic organizations have gained as determinant factors in the U.S. foreign policy establishment.

As Central America continues its path toward greater democratization and participatory policy-making, intermestic policy behavior can be expected to increasingly characterize that region's international behavior as well. While different from the United States in that lobbying is not a common practice, nor is it adequately regulated where it exists, civil society mobilization has become an unavoidable factor when it comes to influencing foreign policy decision-making. Human rights organizations, for instance, played a pivotal role in Guatemala and El Salvador during the democratic transition years immediately following the end of the crisis in the 1980s. In addition, environmental groups deterred and ultimately reversed the Costa Rican government's decision to authorize U.S. companies to carry on petroleum explorations in that country's continental platform. In Panama and Honduras, worker representatives accompanied by their AFL–CIO counterparts have lobbied in the halls of the U.S. Congress against and in favor of the Free Trade Agreement's labor provisions, much to the chagrin of the White House and Central American embassies in Washington.

Before this backdrop, and given the gains achieved by the international civil society movements that have proliferated and thrived on the discontent with the post–Cold War order from Seattle to Porto Alegre, the era of nation-led, Wesphalian diplomacy seems to have experienced significant transformations unforeseen by the Realist School just a few decades ago.

Indeed, globalization and regionalization are major forces that shape this context of change.[5] Globalization has emerged as a major force because of the internationalization and integration of markets, facilitated by advanced information technology. The use of technology has become democratized. Individuals and groups in and out of power now have the ability to instantaneously communicate and share information and interests with similar groups throughout the world. As a consequence, their reach is global. Regionalization has been driven by the growing permeability of borders as well as by the heightened awareness of ethnic, religious, geographic, and economic differences that distinguish one group from another.[6]

The traditional state system of international affairs has weakened significantly. In part it is because states have decreasing control over both their own as well as proximate territories, as the deadly terrorist attacks on 9-11 starkly revealed. The international system is crowded by powerful, nonstate actors, groups, and even individuals, whose reach can be worldwide. They can be as influential as traditional state actors who control a legitimate monopoly over the use of force. We now live in an era where "any place can turn out to be strategic."[7] It is also breached by a range of issues that cannot be resolved on a state-to-state basis, but rather in a multilateral context. In the midst of these changes, the end of the Cold War and the consequent decline in control by the major powers, one observer has boldly stated, "the period from 1990 to 2025/2050 will most likely be short on peace, short on stability, and short on legitimacy."[8]

For Central America, globalization is the leading edge of a boundaryless world market economy that provides rich opportunities as well as significant perils. Key sectors of the Central American economy (traditional and nontraditional agriculture, tourism, and textile assembly) do have some competitiveness beyond regional borders. Others, such as services and high technology, confront greater challenges throughout the region. Whatever the case, globalization promises intensified competition at all levels.

Regionalization has also manifested itself in numerous ways in Central America since the end of the Cold War. In the midst of other regional integration efforts in the Western Hemisphere and in Europe, and with gradual opening to the world market during the past 20 years, there has been a growing consensus about the need for Central America to deepen its own integration efforts as a first step into membership with some of the richer and more powerful blocs. However intense, this consensus remains thwarted by tensions in the region resulting from historical antagonisms, structural reforms, economic and social asymmetries, and sheer lack of political will, both within and among the Central American countries. What is clear for Central America, however, is that it must get beyond its own legitimate issues to demonstrate to the broader policy and market community that it can be serious in its efforts to become part of a larger regional arrangement.

The emergence of a single, global marketplace and regionalization has been accompanied by the growing reality of interdependence and interpenetration between the United States and its hemispheric neighbors. As a result, there has been an erosion of the traditional boundaries between foreign and domestic policy. This erosion has been catalyzed by the end of the great power conflict. Indeed, in the post–Cold War era until 9-11, "national security" had been difficult to define, given the polyarchal nature of the emerging times.

The significant asymmetries that separate the United States from Central America further stress this point. The Central American population represents less than 12% of that of the United States. Its territory amounts to 4.5% of the continental United States. Central America's $65 billion regional GDP equals 0.5% of that of the United States'. Whereas the United States has a per capita income of roughly $35,000 a year, the per capita income in Central America is seven times smaller, a mere $5,100 on the average. Whereas 50% of all Central American exports and more than 50% of all Central American imports are directed to or come from U.S. markets, total Central American trade with the United States only amounts to 1% of its foreign exchange. On average, 38% of the labor force in the isthmus is still engaged in agricultural activities, while in the United States only 1% of the economically active population devotes itself to those tasks. In the World Economic Forum's Competitiveness Index, the United States is in 1st place, Costa Rica in 53rd, El Salvador in 57th, and the rest of the Central American countries between 70 and 75. The United Nations Human Development Index ranks the United States in 6th place, only surpassed by the Nordic countries and Canada. The nearest Central American country is Costa Rica, in 47th place.[9]

In the aftermath of 9-11, the United States has promoted a new global paradigm of antiterrorism and public security. "The enemy is not a single political regime or person or religion or ideology. The enemy is terrorism—premeditated, politically motivated violence perpetrated against innocents."[10] With such a crystal clear definition of threat, fresh on the heels of the catalytic and visually compelling evidence of the terrorist destruction of key social and political icons of U.S. life (the World Trade Center and a wing of the Pentagon), there would be no doubt about the validity of the perceived threat and the new vulnerabilities explicit to the threat.[11]

Thus, globalization and regionalization have brought important changes to the arena of U.S.–Central American affairs in the post–Cold War era. However, 9-11 has been the signal chapter that provides a backdrop that will be to this new era what anticommunism was to the Cold War. What are the general hemispheric trends since the end of the Cold War that inform U.S. –Central American relations?

First, a new and more ambitious hemispheric agenda has been established. The major pillars of this agenda include free trade, democracy, security cooperation, and alternative development. The new agenda is more sensitive to distinct national and regional interests. In the North, Mexico has broken from earlier models of development to open itself to a North American trading bloc. Brazil has emerged as the key force in South America, and after 2003, the emergence of center to left governments throughout the southern cone responds to the growing need for attention to the social question.

Second, since the transition to democracy in Latin America began in the 1980s, many countries have deepened their institutional capacity to govern at the regional and local levels. Throughout the region, this positive trend has produced a second generation of reforms that are enhancing the capacity of countries to be competitive in the global economy and to address critical social and educational needs. Chile is leading the way in this regard.

Third, a new consensus has developed around the necessity for democratic governance, even if there is great uncertainty about the material benefits of democracy. The consensus incorporates new interest in free-market dynamics and increasingly greater concern about inequality, discrimination, and good governance, particularly with regard to corruption, transparency, and accountability. Among other multilateral organizations, the Organization of American States (OAS), the oldest and most important multilateral forum on hemispheric affairs, has promulgated a range of initiatives designed to enhance democratic governance.

Fourth, the emergence of subregional relations since the end of the Cold War has given Latin American countries some additional leverage in their relationships with the United States. In this context, the consolidation of MERCOSUR (the Common Market of the South) as a regional trading bloc in South America balances the regional trading bloc of the north—NAFTA (the North American Free Trade Agreement). Since both arrangements have different philosophical approaches, they emerge as polar choices for countries and regional groups that are weighing the pros and cons of incorporation or accession.[12]

Fifth, as a consequence of 9-11, the Central American security agenda, previously confined to drug trafficking, acquired a new focus and purpose around the issue of terrorism. In the process, the United States has used 9-11 to reconstruct a network of direct working relationships with all military forces throughout the region.

A Region of Diversity

The Central American isthmus is one of the smallest and most diverse regions of the Western Hemisphere. It is formed by seven nation-states (Belize, Guatemala, El Salvador, Honduras, Nicaragua, Costa Rica, and Panama), whose total territorial expanse is similar to that of Texas. It has a total population of 40 million people (twice the size of Florida's), and it extends from Mexico to Colombia, forming a natural bridge that has served as a cultural and environmental passage for thousands of years.

Mestizos, who are the descendants of both native Indian and Spanish individuals, are predominant in Central America. However, the region is still inhabited by indigenous peoples of Mayan ancestry who form the majority of the population in Guatemala and represent a good proportion of Belize's population. Significant Creole or English-speaking communities of African descent live in most of the Caribbean lowlands, where important miscegenation processes with native communities have occurred for hundreds of years.

Sharing a narrow isthmus that is subject to the periodic battering of natural disasters such as violent earthquakes, hurricanes, and volcanic eruptions, the seven sovereign states in the region and their ethnically diverse peoples nevertheless have dissimilar histories and socioeconomic characteristics.

Five countries, Guatemala, El Salvador, Honduras, Nicaragua, and Costa Rica, share either a common pre-Columbian or Hispanic heritage. Their territories were part of the so-called Mesoamerican[13] region, an area later to become part of the Kingdom of Guatemala, an administrative unit of the Viceroyalty of Mexico that gained independence from Spain in 1821. The sixth country, Panama, only obtained its independence from Colombia amidst the U.S. led efforts to build a trans-isthmian canal in 1903. The creation of the Panama Canal Zone under U.S. control and the military occupation that ensued, as well as the adoption of the U.S. dollar as the national currency and the development of a strong, banking and financial services-oriented economy, clearly distinguishes Panama from its northern Central American neighbors. Belize, a colony of Great Britain since the early 1700s, was granted independence in 1981 in spite of the protests and war threats from Guatemala. Until recently, Guatemala considered Belize to be one of its provinces, and even today continues to exert significant, albeit inconsequential, territorial claims over much of a country with which it nevertheless maintains full diplomatic relations. Table 2 compares the six countries that are the subject of this book.

Spiritual and cultural life varies considerably as well. The Roman Catholic Church remains the dominant (and sometimes even official) religion in many Central American countries. However, evangelical churches have expanded significantly throughout the region to the point of nearly surpassing the traditional Catholic majority in Guatemala. Meanwhile, Native and Afro-American cults continue to thrive, making great strides among all social classes, not only within the traditional sectors with which they have been historically associated.

Regional diversity extends into everyday life as well, including sports, music, and food. Most Central Americans consider soccer to be their national sport, yet Nicaraguans and Panamanians prefer baseball, and Belizeans hold firm in their commitment to cricket and rugby. Whereas in northern

Table 2 Central America at a Glance

	Costa Rica	El Salvador	Honduras	Guatemala	Nicaragua	Panama
Area	Smaller than West Virginia	Smaller than Massachusetts	Larger than Tennessee	Smaller than Tennessee	Smaller than New York	Smaller than South Carolina
Population	4.01 million	6.70 million	6.98 million	14.70 million	5.47 million	3.04 million
Life expectancy	76.8 years	71.2 years	65.6 years	65.1 years	70.3 years	71.94 years
Gross domestic product (GDP) (U.S. $)	$37.9 billion	$32.4 billion	$18.79 billion	$59.47 billion	$12.34 billion	$20.57 billion
GDP/per capita (U.S. $)	$9600	$4900	$2800	$4200	$2300	$6900

Source: Data from the *CIA World Factbook*, 2004 at http://www.cia.gov.

Central America, Mexican influences are noticeable from *mariachi* and *grupero* music to the predominance of corn-based diets, in southern and Caribbean Central America rice, tubers, and bread are pervasive, and people dance to the Afro-inspired rhythms of *salsa, merengue,* and *cumbia.*

Differences notwithstanding, this book will focus on the relationships of the six predominantly Spanish-speaking nations of Central America with the United States. These countries, with the exception of Panama, are the founding members of the Central American Common Market. They are also members of the Central American Integration System (SICA) and partners of the Central American Alliance for Sustainable Development (ALIDES), whose relevance will be analyzed in the following pages.

Belize was not included as a major focus of analysis in this book because its historical and political developments are very different from those of its regional neighbors. The fact that Belize was a British colony until 1981 is in itself the most significant differentiating factor but not the only one. While Belize has already joined several important regional undertakings within the loose parameters of the "widened" Central American Integration System (which also includes the Dominican Republic), it is still reluctant to become a full partner of SICA, and not without legitimate reason. The long-standing and unresolved claims of Guatemala over Belizean territory keep the latter at arms length from other Central American countries, and it does enjoy preferential relations with the Caribbean Community and the European Union as a consequence of its former colonial status.

Compelling geopolitical factors allow for Belize's inclusion as a member of the Central American community at large (side by side with the Dominican Republic). Yet we are not convinced that this country can be considered a Central American Republic in the same way other countries in the region clearly are. Most Belizeans would concur with us to this regard.

In this book we assess the major characteristics of U.S.–Central American relations in the aftermath of the Cold War. A dilemma confronted by both the United States and Central America during this period was the rapid disengagement of the United States from the region as a result of movement toward democracy throughout Central America and changing budget and strategic priorities in the United States. This disengagement, however, coincided with the appearance of new issues in the U.S.–Central America agenda including illicit drug traffic, trade negotiations, environmental regulation, and immigration policies, among others. They became important constraints to the relationship throughout the 1990s and into this new century. However, with 9-11, the United States and Central America reverted into a more familiar relationship reminiscent of the Cold War.

We can glean a number of lessons learned from U.S. –Central American matters as they relate to this twenty-first century. These lessons suggest that the United States will continue to be the preponderant geopolitical force in Central America in this new century. However, for the region, preponderance does not and should not always mean submission. Indeed, Central America now has a range of options for establishing bilateral and multilateral relations outside of direct U.S. influence and control.

While subject to the principal U.S. concern for security and antiterrorism, the contention of this book is that Central America must take advantage of these new opportunities to reap the benefits of the new, globalized, international economy. The book suggests the elements that will be necessary to foster a more thoughtful and productive relationship between Central America and its powerful neighbor to the north. It also explores the likely configuration of a future greater Caribbean area, whose internal dynamics, and ultimately geopolitical configuration, will probably differ significantly from the current one. To this regard, the book provides some notions of the kinds of new national and regional interactions that will take place within a context of enhanced technological means, broader trade understandings, and weaker nineteenth century concepts of state sovereignty.

Overall, this book approaches U.S.–Central American relations from a pragmatic as well as an optimistic viewpoint. It acknowledges the abysmal military, economic, and technological divide that exists between the United States and the isthmus, yet it also perceives the opportunities that those asymmetries tend to obscure. After all, democratic consolidation, institutional build-up, sustainable development, economic growth, and the construction of a truly transparent and accountable political culture are common objectives that the United States and the Central American Republics share. They constitute the patrimony of well-being and prosperity (without which the whole region's long-term stability would be at risk) and the source for hope in an era too often driven by fear and selfishness.

CHAPTER 1

Is the Past Prologue to the Future?

Introduction[1]

Central America has been an area of preponderant influence of the United States since the late 1800s. Yet, U.S. interest in Central America has been greatly overestimated by unjustified perceptions of threat to U.S. national security. Indeed, U.S. concerns over real or imagined third-party intrusions in Central America have been more psychological than strategic. Although the region possesses some geopolitical points of value, such as the Panama Canal or an eventual trans-isthmus corridor linking the world through sophisticated transportation and communications networks, the isthmus has tended to have marginal significance to U.S. national security.[2]

U.S. foreign policy decision-making toward Central America can be characterized by cycles of intervention and neglect, as Table 1.1 illustrates.[3] Neglect does not mean oblivion, however, for the United States never ignored its southern neighbors altogether. Yet, U.S. preponderance has not always been exercised with equal force, mainly owing to specific historical conditions that will be analyzed later in greater detail. Those cycles, which occur regardless of the ideological preference of the administration in power, have prevented the development of a sound, long-term relationship based on mutually beneficial objectives. They also have allowed the United States to exercise its preponderance through either direct military domination or more subtle yet equally effective mechanisms derived from its overwhelming economic and political influence.[4]

Table 1.1 The United States in Central America (1898–2005): Cycles of Intervention and Neglect

Period	Presidents	Nature of Cycle	Main Events
1898–1933	William McKinley Theodore Roosevelt William H. Taft Woodrow Wilson Warren Harding Calvin Coolidge Herbert C. Hoover Franklin D. Roosevelt	Intervention	Spanish-American War. Monroe Corollary to the Monroe Doctrine. Dollar Diplomacy. Gunboat Diplomacy: repeated interventions in Nicaragua, Honduras, the Dominican Republic, and Haiti. The United States goes to war in Europe. Sandino fights guerrilla war.
1933–1946	Franklin D. Roosevelt Harry S. Truman	Neglect	The United States recuperates from world financial collapse. FDR enacts New Deal. The United States prepares and then goes to war. World War II. Alliance with the Soviet Union to fight Nazism. In Central America, the United States supports military dictators.
1947–1989	Harry S. Truman Dwight D. Eisenhower John F. Kennedy Lyndon B. Johnson Richard M. Nixon Gerald R. Ford James (Jimmy) E. Carter Ronald Reagan George H. W. Bush	Intervention	The Cold War. National Security Doctrine. Cuban Revolution. Vietnam. Counter insurgency campaigns. Guerrillas appear in Guatemala, El Salvador, and Nicaragua. Somoza is ousted. Soviet Union intervenes in Afghanistan and Africa with Cuban support. Contention evolves into "roll back." Massive military support to El Salvador to fight against FMLN; U.S. finances the Contras in Nicaragua. Central America Peace Plan (Esquipulas II) is signed. U.S. invasion of Panama.
1990–1997	George H. W. Bush William J. Clinton	Neglect	End of the Cold War. Fall of the Berlin Wall. The Soviet Union collapses. Sandinistas lose elections in Nicaragua. The former Yugoslavia torn apart by ethnic and national wars. The United States is involved in Somalia, the Balkans, and Middle East.
1997–2007 (ongoing)	William J. Clinton George W. Bush	Intervention	Plan Colombia is enacted. Terrorist attacks on the United States. U.S. invasion of Afghanistan and Iraq. Patriot Act.

Throughout the Cold War, real, perceived, and even exaggerated threats to U.S. national security were used as a tool for domestic purposes.[5] An illustrative example of the exaggerated importance attributed to the Cold War in U.S. foreign policy visions can be found in John Updike's novel, *Rabbit at Rest,* when one of the characters off-handedly asks, "Without the Cold War, what's the point of being an American?"[6] This would be further stressed even when the fears of bipolar confrontation ebbed at the end of the 1980s. Reflecting upon an international system plagued with confusion and global disarray, and confronted with the inevitable rise of the United States as the sole superpower, Samuel Huntington said, "A nation's interests derive from its identity. But without an enemy to define itself against, America's identity has disintegrated."[7]

In the case of Central America, the United States tried to justify its preference for unilateral actions in a region considered its "backyard" by using the specter of communism. This strategy allowed the United States to maintain the *Pax Americana* for well over 50 years while at the same time arguing that this was necessary to defend and protect major U.S. national interests. Thus, U.S. policies toward Central America evolved into an agenda dominated by fear and oriented toward the maintenance of the status quo. This agenda featured military action and political repression to counteract those perceived threats, which in times of neglect were narrowly focused, if at all, on short-term development and humanitarian issues.

The United States only became interested in Central America in the mid-nineteenth century, particularly owing to the growing need for a canal passage through the isthmus. At the time, the discovery of gold in California (1848) had put a significant strain on land transportation, as thousands of gold seekers rushed to the West, and a faster, safer passage through Nicaragua became crucial. The rising importance of transcontinental transportation, and later the ill-fated military adventures of Confederate entrepreneurs looking for the expansion of their plantation economy to Central America under the leadership of William Walker, generated unprecedented attention on the isthmus, particularly among important members of the East Coast elites.

It was not until after 1906 that the proliferation of American investments in the region, resulting in banana plantations expanding in Honduras and Costa Rica and the development of notable mining enterprises in Nicaragua, justified official U.S. government involvement in the region on a significant scale. The construction of the Panama Canal (inaugurated in 1913), and the establishment of military installations in the Canal Zone beginning that same year, undoubtedly signaled the definitive strategic positioning of the United States in the isthmus. By the end of the World

War I, the United States had firmly supplanted Europe as the region's major trading and investment partner.

Recurring U.S. military incursions into Nicaragua and Honduras, including the occupation of the former between 1909 and 1933, as well as the implementation of Dollar Diplomacy through the 1920s and 1930s, furthered U.S. influence in Central America. This was enhanced by the assumption of power of autocratic military regimes in all countries of the region except Costa Rica. The appearance of the first anarchist and socialist parties inspired by the Mexican (1910) and Bolshevik (1917) revolutions, and the rise of nationalistic movements such as the combative army of Augusto Cesar Sandino in Nicaragua, became early, and sometimes even successful, adversaries of U.S. policies in the region.

During the World War II, once a few outbursts of fascist sympathies among Central American presidents (civilian and military alike) were put to rest, the United States and the region's governments maintained a solid military and diplomatic alliance. Once the conflict was over, and the Iron Curtain had divided Europe after 1947, the dictatorial regimes supported by the United States in Central America became strengthened as the result of fears of the spread of communism. While this was a common trait in the Western Hemisphere as a whole, one salient example of this was the U.S.-sponsored ouster of an elected reform-minded president of Guatemala in 1954. The U.S.-led doctrine of national security during the 1960s culminated this phase of strategic submission, which included, most notably, the participation of Central American soldiers in the U.S.-led intervention in the Dominican Republic in 1964.

The submissive trend during the 1970s was punctuated by several exceptions: a decision taken only by Costa Rica to normalize diplomatic relations with the Soviet Union and other socialist countries in 1971; the tensions between the Guatemalan Armed Forces and the Carter Administration (1976–1980) over human rights issues in the country; and the 1977 turnover of the Panama Canal from U.S. control to the government of Panama as a consequence of treaty obligations and a retrenchment of the U.S. military presence in the face of rising costs.[8]

Yet the dominant trend continued to manifest itself in Nicaragua and El Salvador. Throughout the 1970s, military-backed governments in both countries resisted reform, a shortsighted decision that resulted in escalating political and military crises that ultimately led to civil war.

The Central American crisis (1979–1989) strengthened the ties between the United States and its regional political and military allies in all the countries of Central America except Nicaragua. It also inaugurated a phase of intense interventionism under the aegis of the "rollback" doctrine of the Reagan Administration. In the words of President Reagan,

"We must stand by all our democratic allies. And we must not break faith with those who are risking their lives—on every continent, from Afghanistan to Nicaragua—to defy Soviet-supported aggression and secure rights which have been ours from birth."[9]

This approach to foreign policy posited that communist revolutions not only had to be contained, but also could and should be reversed. To this end, the United States would support local democratic insurgencies (the so-called freedom fighters) that were financed, trained, and equipped by the Central Intelligence Agency (CIA) in Afghanistan, Angola, Mozambique, and Nicaragua—a country where they became a powerful yet unruly and ultimately unsuccessful irregular army popularly known as the "Contra." For the United States and its president, this was not only justified, but also consistent with international practices. Indeed, in requesting support for these irregular armies in Central America, President Reagan proclaimed, "The Sandinista dictatorship of Nicaragua, with full Cuban-Soviet bloc support, not only persecutes its people, the church, and denies a free press, but arms and provides bases for Communist terrorists attacking neighboring states. Support for freedom fighters is self-defense and totally consistent with the Organization of American States (OAS) and the United Nations (UN) Charters. It is essential that the Congress continue all facets of our assistance to Central America. I want to work with you to support the democratic forces whose struggle is tied to our own security."[10]

In Honduras, for example, a country whose military leadership was able to manage a modest democratic opening, the United States built the Palmerola Air Base in 1981. This base became a valuable military asset for U.S.-backed "freedom fighters," but would also prove essential for American logistics in the isthmus throughout the decade and beyond as the U.S. military bases in Panama closed.

U.S. policy toward Central America during this period was directly conditioned by at least two U.S. domestic factors:

- The failure of the Contra option and the rupture of the consensus between the White House and Congress over U.S. strategies in Central America once the Iran-Contra scandal was disclosed.[11]
- The election of President George Bush in 1988. As the Soviet Union declined and the end of the Cold War became apparent, President Bush's international priorities quickly shifted from Central America to Europe and the Middle East. This also coincided with the successful implementation of the Esquipulas Peace Plan and its most significant outcome: the defeat of the Nicaraguan leftist *Sandinistas* in the 1990 elections.[12]

From Hegemonic Predominance to Relative Autonomy

The United States has enjoyed a position of predominance over Central America largely justified by the Monroe Doctrine of 1823 and the Roosevelt Corollary of 1906.[13] However, it is possible to find periods in history when such predominance has been weakened and Central America has been able to enjoy larger degrees of relative autonomy. This relative autonomy can be defined as the capability of the countries in the region to exercise their foreign policy agendas without the constraints imposed by and even in spite of, the United States' own geopolitical interests.

Since 1933, there have been two situations when Central America, and Latin America in general, has been able to gain greater independence *vis à vis* the hegemonic power. The first situation results from the rupture of bipartisan consensus over foreign policy in the United States as a consequence of isolationist tendencies and domestic concerns that overshadow international, geopolitical priorities. When the U.S. domestic situation allows the executive and the legislative branches to forge a foreign policy consensus under presidential leadership, U.S. preponderance increases. When dissention prevails or the credibility of the administration is at stake, the margins of autonomy of foreign actors widens significantly. One expression of enhanced margins of autonomy in Central America is the willingness of the United States to admit (and even foster) multilateral participation in the region. Seldom does a hegemon agree to third-party intervention in its areas of influence. Equally, it mistrusts and generally rejects the multilateral approach because it deprives or lessens significantly its direct intervention capacity.

In the Caribbean, the United States has been willing to support multilateral intervention (particularly that of the UN) when experiencing phases of disinterest or neglect, such as those in Haiti or Central America after 1987. The OAS, an institution generally regarded as an instrument of the United States, was a preferred choice even at times of intervention. This notwithstanding, OAS activism in Central America has heightened and shown more autonomy and creativity in moments of neglect, such as the early 1990s.

The second situation is external. It is triggered by a significant event in the international arena such as the World War II, the "thaw" between the United States and the Soviet Union in the mid-1970s, or the demise of the Soviet Empire and economic globalization during the 1990s. In those cases the international climate drives the United States to adopt a more flexible hemispheric policy in the certainty that it would not threaten its national security objectives.[14] When this occurs, third parties such as multilateral institutions (the UN, the OAS) or even countries generally viewed as unwelcome intruders in the Americas, are either allowed, or even encouraged, to participate in regional affairs. This was clearly the case during the unraveling of the Esquipulas peace process, when the UN, the OAS, and the European Union became significant actors in the implementation phases of the regional agreements without the U.S. Administration being able to object to their newly acquired influence in the area.

Contention, Repression, and Underdevelopment

Just as ensuring internal stability became the motto for U.S. military interventions in the Caribbean Basin at the turn of the century, the "communist threat" was Washington's justification to maintain its regional hegemony after 1947. This perception constituted the core of the U.S. National Security Doctrine, whose implementation delayed Central American development and produced some of the worst human rights violations in the history of the hemisphere.

During the late 1970s, Central America experienced the radicalization and public mobilization of leftist political parties and popular movements.[15] Many of these organizations, especially those affiliated with the doctrinal line of the Soviet Union, had appeared in the 1920s and 1930s, influenced by the tenets of the Mexican Revolution and "proletarian internationalism," the world revolutionary doctrine introduced by Lenin at the Third International.[16] Brutally repressed during the peasant upheaval of 1932 in El Salvador, and systematically persecuted by the Somoza dictatorship in Nicaragua since 1933, these parties and workers' unions gained added credibility in the wake of the U.S. alliance with the Soviet Union during the World War II. In Costa Rica and Guatemala, communists played a central role in the social reforms of the 1940s and 1950s, supporting the social doctrine of the Roman Catholic Church and the unprecedented reformist proposals implemented under the aegis of the enlightened national bourgeoisies.[17]

Those reforms, nevertheless, were only possible because of short-lived, conjunctural alliances. In the aftermath of the World War II, the socialist and communist movements of Central America suffered a renewed phase of repression and persecution. In Costa Rica, the Civil War of 1948 did not reverse the social reforms achieved peacefully with communist support between 1942 and 1946. Yet the 1949 Constitution outlawed the Communist Party (the prohibition was maintained, but not enforced, until 1970), and many of its leaders were compelled to leave or stay out of the country. In Guatemala the reformist experiment lasted a decade (1944–1954). Then the social democratic coalition of Jacobo Arbenz was ousted from power in a bloody coup with the open intervention of the CIA and the United Fruit Company, whose economic interests were threatened by the land reform.[18]

The creation of the Inter-American Treaty of Reciprocal Assistance (TIAR, or Rio Treaty of 1947) was the origin of what would 15 years later become the National Security Doctrine. This binding, international instrument defined communism as an extra-continental threat subject to collective action. A predecessor of the North Atlantic Treaty Organization (NATO) and the South East Asia Treaty Organization (SEATO), the TIAR was the legal framework upon which an age of uncontested U.S. hegemony over Latin America would rest for over four decades.

Fidel Castro's revolutionary triumph in Cuba in 1959, that country's formal alliance with the Soviet Union after 1961, and Cuba's support of insurrectional movements throughout Latin America in the 1970s increased the persecution and repression of communist movements in Central America. The Cuban Revolution also motivated the enactment of the Alliance for Progress by the Kennedy administration, whose stated objectives were to foster democracy and reduce economic and social inequalities through modernization.[19] While the goals of the Alliance for Progress were reform-oriented—with the exception of Costa Rica—the program was only partially implemented because of stern opposition from the region's elites and their military surrogates.

From Authoritarian Contention to Democratic Promotion

The Central American crisis of the 1980s systematically eroded the principles underlying the Monroe Doctrine and the Roosevelt Corollary. The combination of poverty and repression that dominated Central America during the 1960s and 1970s, as well as the indisputable influence and support of the Cuban Revolution, explain the radicalization of the political left, which managed to form semicohesive fronts during the early 1970s. Only then did they begin to organize systematic military actions against the ruling military elites and their social allies. These actions, which were quasi-criminal and very localized at first (kidnappings, bank robberies, burning and bombing of properties, etc.), soon became military operations carried out throughout the countries with extraordinary popular and international support. In less than a decade the incipient and fractious insurrection movements of El Salvador turned guerrilla incursions into a full-fledged civil war that almost toppled the long-standing "14 families" who ruled the country behind a façade of fraudulent elections. In Nicaragua the rebels were even able to overthrow a dynastic dictator and rule the country for over 10 years.

In Guatemala, ironically the country with the oldest guerrilla movement of the region, the rebels were never able to become a major threat to the political system. Yet they constituted a constant irritation to the ruling military that lasted for over 30 years, amidst some of the most brutal human rights violations in the history of Latin America, some of which were genocidal in nature. In Honduras a reform-oriented military initiated land distribution, thereby largely defusing significant political tensions. As a result, the Cinchonero Movement and the Morazanista Front only carried out isolated urban assaults of small political consequence. In the process organized labor and student movements were decimated by disappearances and government-sponsored death squad activity. Costa Rica also suffered important social mobilizations, but its stronger institutions and long-standing civilian and democratic tradition were capable of neutralizing the few instances in which minuscule military cells (mostly rejected even by the main socialist parties) attempted revolutionary outcomes in the early 1980s.

For the United States, the appearance of *guerrilla* fronts throughout Central America, and the discovery of their doctrinal and logistic linkages to Cuba, became irrefutable proof of a communist plot, designed in Moscow and Havana. Perceived under the logic of the Cold War and spurred by the Reagan doctrine of "roll-back," the conflict in Central America soon became a test case for Washington. In Washington's view, it not only defied Western democracy and threatened what former Secretary of State Alexander Haig called "America's soft underbelly," but it also questioned some of the most cherished premises of the Monroe Doctrine so jealously kept since 1823.

The U.S. response was swift and decisive. The military governments and the Central American armed forces enjoyed almost unrestrained access to logistic and technical support from the Pentagon and the CIA. During this period, American military advisors systematically trained the armed and police forces of the region, both in-country, as well as at the School of the Americas in the Panama Canal Zone. They also provided military equipment under the premise—cornerstone of the TIAR—that extra-continental aggression toward one member of the Inter-American system (and communism qualified in that category) should be considered an act of aggression against all.[20]

This partnership was devastating for Central American democracy in at least three ways. First, it strengthened the military and their dictatorial governments to the detriment of civilian leaders, political parties, and other nongovernmental organizations such as unions and rural cooperatives. Lacking solid, democratic structures, most countries of Central America could not and would not uphold the rule of law for many decades.

Second, American support of the military promoted—either directly or by omission—massive violations of human rights committed under a policy of state-sponsored terrorism by the armed forces or indirectly through paramilitary organizations with strong ties to the army and extremist right-wing parties. Third, it impeded social and economic development. Indeed, in defining almost any reform as a communist-inspired threat to the status quo, the application of the National Security Doctrine in Central America inhibited the possibility of gradual changes that could have probably prevented the social explosions that devastated the isthmus.[21]

It would be a simplification, however, to attribute to the United States or to American companies with business interests in Central America the main responsibility for the poverty and lack of democracy in the isthmus. While Washington's security policies contributed decisively to the establishment and maintenance of military regimes in the region since the 1930s, local elites had numerous opportunities throughout the twentieth century to open their political and economic systems. In Costa Rica they did; in the rest of Central America they did not. Hence, in large part, those ultra-conservative elites who resisted reform are also to be held responsible for the unfair and discriminatory nature of their countries' political, economic, and social structures, and in large part for the political turmoil and suffering they brought on their citizens once war broke loose.[22]

U.S. security and business practices did not operate in a regional political and social vacuum. On the contrary, they found in Central America a realm dominated by landowners and national bourgeoisies that thrived in political systems characterized by undemocratic and exploitative traditions. For decades these groups exercised control over the armed forces, upon which they bestowed the responsibility of the administration of their interests. This understanding nourished the emergence of a symbiotic relationship between those who ruled and those who governed in their name. This relationship would not be altered until after the politico-military crisis of the 1980s.[23]

Ironically, the Central American crisis allowed the military to become independent from their original patrons. Strengthened by the generous assistance of a fearful United States, and enriched by unbridled corruption, the armed forces of the region became businessmen in uniform, devoted to lucrative activities that included cement factories, banks, soccer teams, funeral homes, and airlines. One salient enterprise was the administration of substantial pension funds, whose benefits became the source of even further economic activities, sometimes beyond national borders. In the process, sometimes they displaced the traditional economic elites while at the same time keeping tight control over government institutions, which they used for their own economic enhancement.[24] The United

States acknowledged and was sometimes mortified by these peculiar relationships. Through the years, Washington tried unsuccessfully to induce reforms in the national systems that could engender what became known as "low-intensity democracies." One early example of those moments came during the years of the Alliance for Progress, when Washington went as far as to propose programs of taxation and land reform that were immediately rebuked by the ruling elites. Another breakthrough came during the Carter administration, when the United States unilaterally decided to interrupt U.S. military assistance to Guatemala because of its dismal human rights record. American ostracism did not prevent the Guatemalan military from carrying out their brutal repressive practices with the expertise and logistic support of Argentina, Chile, and Israel.[25]

Even with this recognition, Washington could not resist the pressure to use Central America as a geopolitical peon in its Cold War chess game, especially upon Ronald Reagan's election as President in 1981.[26] On the one hand, the U.S. reformist and democratic efforts were neither systematic nor consistent throughout the region (for example, the United States never interrupted its military assistance to El Salvador or Honduras, where human rights violations were pervasive and well known to U.S. policymakers in Washington and in the field). On the other hand, it took years for the United States to acknowledge the "structural" nature of the Central American crisis, namely, the fact that while there were undoubtedly foreign factors (such as Cuban intervention and Soviet block support) that were irritating it, the crisis itself had brewed for decades, having its roots deeply entrenched in domestic, historically specific social and economic inequalities.[27]

The predominance of a highly ideological reading of regional events by the United States, coupled with a strong reluctance to allow a peaceful, nonmilitary solution in an area considered to be under its exclusive hegemonic control, inhibited a timely, negotiated settlement of the Central American crisis. It also put the United States in a no-win situation. Indeed, by 1984 the Department of State was forced to recognize the structural nature of the crisis, while at the same time being proven unable to prevent the political dialogue initiatives started in Central America under the auspices of the Contadora Group and the European Union.[28]

Thus, the isolated reformist and modernization efforts sponsored by Washington in Central America after 1976 were neither timely nor effective. They almost always took place once the historical circumstances and the cumulative impact of U.S. actions made it virtually impossible to introduce significant changes in the political system. This happened, for example, with the unsuccessful attempts of the Carter administration to control the downfall of Anastasio Somoza in Nicaragua in 1979, by trying to broker an eleventh-hour mechanism that would have produced a

"Somoza-ism without Somoza." This was also the case of the Reagan administration's futile efforts to build viable democracies in Honduras and El Salvador in 1983 and 1984. Not even more integral and sophisticated attempts, such as the 1984 final report of the President's National Bipartisan Commission on Central America (better known as the Kissinger Commission Report), were capable of giving the system the stability it had lost after many decades of neglect and political mismanagement (see Table 1.2).[29]

This two-tiered policy was ineffective not only because of timing, but also because it was not credible. The Reagan Administration's preference for a military rather than a political solution to the Central American conflict was evident to all the parties involved, including the UN, the OAS, the European Union, and the Latin American countries. For all of the Kissinger Commission's high profile, its mandate was always obscured (and in many ways undermined) by covert operations and clandestine support to the Nicaraguan Contras and to the brutal Salvadoran Armed Forces.

Thus, what the U.S. State Department portrayed as a two-track approach to the regional crisis was understood by the rest of the world to be a mere cover-up of the White House, the CIA, and the National Security Council's real intention: achieving a decisive military victory in Nicaragua and El Salvador. This apparent contradiction between rhetoric and reality—and its worse consequence, a seemingly deceptive stratagem aimed at misleading the international community—became the most persuasive argument for Contadora and the European Union to carry on their diplomatic mediation in Central America against Washington's designs.

The Kissinger Commission's efforts were aimed at producing a much-needed updating and transformation of Central American economies and political regimes. This was to be achieved along the lines of the democratic reforms espoused by the Alliance for Progress a quarter century before, including a significant provision of U.S. financial assistance. In the words of its chairman, former Secretary of State Henry A. Kissinger, "The turmoil in Central America is, undoubtedly, not caused originally by Moscow or Havana. There are many local causes: social injustice, inequality, and historic legacy. Those causes have to be removed."[30] So high were the expectations generated by the Commission, that some believe it would become a true "Marshall Plan for Central America," supported by as much as $20 billion in aid. All those expectations would prove exaggerated and the efforts futile. Neither the reform nor the political will and resources needed to produce it would be forthcoming.

One important exception to this trend was the Caribbean Basin Initiative (CBI), a proposal that emanated from the Kissinger Commission recommendations (see Table 1.3). The CBI was conceived as a program

Table 1.2 Selected Kissinger Commission Report Recommendations Pertaining to Economic and Social Development

An Emergency Stabilization Program

A comprehensive approach to the economic development of the region and the reinvigoration of the Central American Common Market

Involvement of the private sector

Addressing the external debt problem

Immediate increase in bilateral economic assistance

Investing expanded aid in labor infrastructure and housing

Making available new official trade credit guarantees

The United States should join the Central American Bank of Economic Integration

Providing an emergency credit to the Central American Common Market Fund

A Medium Long-Term Reconstruction and Development Plan

Elimination of the climate of violence and civil strife

Development of democratic institutions and processes

Development of strong and free economies and diversified production for both the external and domestic markets

Sharp improvement in the social conditions of the poorest Central Americans

Substantially improved distribution of income and wealth

Human Development

Reduction of malnutrition

Elimination of illiteracy

Universal access to primary education

Universal access to primary health

A significant reduction of infant mortality

Sustained reduction in population growth rates

Significant improvement in housing

Educational Opportunities

Expansion of the Peace Corps' recruitment of front-line teachers to serve in the new Literacy Corps

Expansion of the Peace Corps at the primary, secondary, and technical levels, in part by establishing a Central American Teacher Corps recruited from the Spanish-speaking population of the United States

An expanded program of secondary-level technical and vocational education

Expansion of the International Executive Service Corps (IESC)

Table 1.2 Selected Kissinger Commission Report Recommendations Pertaining to Economic and Social Development (continued)

A program of 10,000 government-sponsored scholarships to bring Central American students to the United States

A long-term plan to strengthen the major universities in Central America

A greatly expanded effort, subsidized by the U.S. government through the National Endowment for the Humanities to train high-level translators, to support translations of important books from both languages, and to subsidize their publication to make them generally available

Source: *The Report of the President's National Bipartisan Commission on Central America*, New York: MacMillan Publishing Company, 1984.

of unilateral trade preferences given by the United States to the Central American and Caribbean democratic countries to enhance and facilitate their exports to the highly protective U.S. markets. Through the years, the CBI became a powerful foreign policy tool but also an indispensable development opportunity for all the economies of the region.[31]

As the regional crisis deepened throughout the 1980s, and given the massive American involvement in the conflict in Nicaragua, Honduras, and El Salvador, more and more extra-regional actors (state and multilateral, official and private) engaged in activities that gradually foreclosed Washington's options in the area.[32]

A first rupture occurred with the formation of the Group of Contadora at the end of 1983. This Group formed by Colombia, Mexico, Panama, and Venezuela was created to prevent a direct U.S. military intervention in Nicaragua similar to the one that had just happened in Grenada earlier that same year. The biggest contribution of the Group of Contadora, and later of its Support Group (Argentina, Brazil, Peru, and Uruguay) to the pacification of Central America was the neutralization of such a scenario, which would have probably spread the hostilities throughout the region.[33]

The diversification of Central American international linkages was also enhanced by the decision of the European Community to establish a permanent political forum with the governments of the region and the members of the Contadora Group as observers. The so-called Dialogue of San Jose, established in 1984 in the capital city of Costa Rica, had among its main objectives preempting the expansion of the war. Differently from Contadora and its Support Group, the European initiative not only called for self-determination and nonintervention, but also sponsored democratic development, namely the establishment of pluralistic, freely elected regimes under the rule of law. This important condition, directly aimed at preventing the expansion of the Nicaraguan revolutionary model or the consolidation of a single-party Marxist government in El Salvador, would eventually become one of the main pillars of the Esquipulas Peace Plan.[34]

Table 1.3 Selected Features of the Caribbean Basin Initiative (CBI)

The Reagan Administration created the program as a perk for nations that sided with the United States in Cold War politics and demonstrated commitment to freemarket principles. The Caribbean Basin Initiative is not a trade agreement. Rather, it is a nonreciprocal grant, by statute of a Cold War anticommunism commercial program that was extended in 1999 providing special duty-free access to the U.S. market for textiles, apparel, and other goods made in the 24-country CBI region.

The CBI region includes the Central American countries of Belize, Costa Rica, El Salvador, Guatemala, Guyana, Honduras, Nicaragua, and Panama, as well as the following Caribbean island nations: Antigua, Aruba, the Bahamas, Barbados, British Virgin Islands, Dominica, Dominican Republic, Grenada, Haiti, Jamaica, Montserrat, Netherlands Antilles, St. Kitts and Nevis, St. Lucia, St. Vincent and the Grenadines, and Trinidad and Tobago.

The trade programs of the Caribbean Basin Initiative remain a vital element in the United States' economic relations with its neighbors in Central America and the Caribbean. The CBI is intended to facilitate the economic development and export diversification of the Caribbean Basin economies. Initially launched in 1983 through the Caribbean Basin Economic Recovery Act (CBERA), and substantially expanded in 2000 through the U.S.–Caribbean Basin Trade Partnership Act (CBTPA), the CBI currently provides 24 beneficiary countries with duty-free access to the U.S. market for most goods.

CBTPA became effective on October 1, 2000 and continues in effect until September 30, 2008, or the date, if sooner, on which the FTAA or another free trade agreement as described in legislation comes into effect between the United States and a CBTPA beneficiary country.

There are currently 24 countries that benefit from the CBI program and, therefore, may potentially benefit from CBTPA. The CBTPA will be up for renewal in 2007.

Source: See Global Citizen page of *The Public Citizen* http://www.citizen.org/trade/cafta/.

By 1985 U.S. policy in Central America was in a quagmire. The White House and the Department of State were increasingly isolated from the Congress and public opinion. Furthermore, incapable of defeating the rebels in El Salvador and unable to topple the Nicaraguan revolutionary government, the United States was reaping all the problems, and not the benefits, of its ill-designed regional policy. This was worsened by the wave of international criticism coming from foes and friends alike and by the very real danger of an extension of the conflict owing to the U.S.-sponsored counter-revolutionary platforms installed in Honduras and Costa Rica by rogue U.S. military operatives (individuals such as former U.S. Marine Oliver North),[35] who illegally used the White House and his relationship with President Reagan to support the Nicaraguan Contras—to the subsequent embarrassment of the Reagan administration.

When the Iran-Contra scandal broke loose in mid-1986, it was all too clear that Washington was alone in a battle that could not be won according to the terms outlined five years earlier by the Group of Santa Fe, formed by Reagan's inner circle—Less so, given the unexpected events triggered by Mikhail Gorbachov's *perestroika* and *glasnost*, which began the downfall of the Soviet empire and heralded the end of the Cold War.

In less than 15 months, between May 1986 and August 1987, Central America emerged from war and violence into the negotiation of a peace plan. This dramatic evolution resulted from a series of regional events associated with internal as well as external circumstances. Among the most significant of these circumstances:

- The uncovering of the Iran-Contra scandal and its impact on the credibility of the White House before Congress and the U.S. public opinion.
- The beginning of political reform in the Soviet Union and the rapprochement between the Washington and Moscow after the Malta Summit.
- The tactical deadlock between the government forces and the rebel groups in El Salvador and Nicaragua.
- The unviability of the Contadora Group proposal for peace in Central America and the proposal of the Arias Plan as a better alternative.
- The economic costs and negative impacts of the war upon the Central American elites after more than a decade of conflict.
- The increasing pressures of the international community over the regional and extra-regional actors involved in the crisis.
- The coming about of democratically elected civilian governments in several countries of the region that were formerly ruled by military dictatorships.
- The election of George H. W. Bush and the advent of a more pragmatic team of foreign policy advisors in the State Department and the National Security Council.

In this new historical circumstance, U.S. policy evolved from diplomatic sabotage of any peace efforts, to explicit skepticism, to reluctant admission, and finally into constructive engagement. This transition occurred as the negotiations of the peace plan proceeded. While this occurred, it became clearer that the objectives so ardently pursued by the Reagan Administration by military means would probably be more legitimate, better served, and more easily achieved through the use of traditional, multilateral diplomatic channels.

The successful culmination of the peace negotiations in August 1987 took the executive branch of the U.S. Government by surprise. The absence of a nonmilitary alternative to the White House's design forced the State Department to take part in a scenario in which it was not prepared to perform. After recovering from the early paralysis produced by the unexpected signing of the peace plan, the White House became entangled in its own contradictions. Unable to reject the negotiation alltogether without becoming completely isolated from the rest of the world, the State Department accepted it reluctantly, but not before expressing serious reservations about the feasibility of its implementation.[36]

In practice, though, this meant the United States would keep its regional policy virtually unchanged. Furthermore, as the critical deadlines of the plan's calendar drew near, the strategy followed by the White House became apparent. The failure of the peace plan had to be portrayed as a self-fulfilling prophesy, an indisputable proof of the lack of political will and cynicism of the Nicaraguan government and the leftist rebels in El Salvador and Guatemala.

By late 1987 the momentum reached in the negotiations and the presence of the United Nations, the OAS, and other parties as verifying institutions of the agreement had severely hampered American political and diplomatic maneuvering. Washington's decision not to suspend its military and humanitarian support to the Nicaraguan Contras and the continuation of military aid to El Salvador and Honduras would ultimately prove counterproductive to U.S. objectives in the region.[37]

By deciding not to join the peace process wholeheartedly, but at the same time incapable of producing a better alternative to end the crisis, the United States lost a unique opportunity to become a part of the solution and go on the offensive. Moreover, it deepened the perception that it was as much a cause of the regional crisis as Cuba, the USSR, and the indigenous insurgent movements. Turned for all practical purposes into a culprit by its own allies' determination to uphold their peace plan regardless of its protests, Washington became entrapped amidst an increasing barrage of international pressures.

While the peace plan got underway in Central America with enormous logistic and political difficulties, the collapse of communist governments in Eastern Europe captured most of the United States' attention. The end of the Cold War would bring about a significant transformation in U.S.–Central American relations. After all, the guiding logic for the U.S. presence in the region was driven by the perceived threat of "another Cuba."

Facing an inevitable negotiation of the crisis in Central America, the United States adopted a two-pronged strategy. Its first component remained military and was aimed at maintaining the pressure on the Sandinista government through the counter revolutionary forces based in Honduras, as well as upon the Salvadoran FMLN rebels through direct military support to the Salvadoran Army. In the case of Nicaragua, the U.S. Congress forced the White House to stop "lethal" aid and only provide "humanitarian" support to the Contras. Yet it was well known that the rebel forces had enough material in stock and would continue to receive enough logistic and intelligence support to carryout their military operations through 1989. In El Salvador, while Congress compelled the administration to adopt measures aimed at ensuring greater compliance of the Armed Forces with respect to human rights, American military support did not dwindle until after a peace agreement was signed in 1992.

The second component was political and diplomatic. Its objective was to promote and strengthen democracy and democratic values through free, fair, and internationally supervised elections. Democratic development had been an important but ultimately secondary concern of U.S. foreign policy during the Cold War. With the deterioration and decline of Soviet-style governance in both the USSR and Eastern Europe, the United States fostered pro-democracy initiatives focused on party development, administration of justice, and electoral reform aimed at Eastern Europe and Central America.

Everybody knew that once the peace plan was signed, Nicaragua would become its principal test case. While all the signing parties were called to comply with the terms and principles of the plan in identical conditions, it was clear that in reality the Sandinista regime was going to be held to much higher standards.

This resulted from at least four specific conditions: first, the nature of the Sandinista regime, whose ideology favored the predominance of a single-party, highly centralized executive supported by an equally partisan armed force; second, the reluctance of the Sandinistas to hold free and fair elections and to fully respect human rights (especially political and individual liberties); third, the fact that all the other Central American governments, imperfect and unrepresentative as they were, had been legitimized by internationally supervised elections, and therefore considered that they could be exempted from some of the Peace Plan obligations. Finally, by the late 1980s, the collapse of the USSR and its Eastern European client states effectively ended the consequential material and moral support that had underwritten Sandinista policy initiatives throughout the decade.

The Sandinistas also had internal reasons that compelled them to admit their regime's singular scrutiny, even when this put them in an untenable situation and ultimately made them lose political power. Just as the United States was being pressured by the international community to abide by the peace plan, so were the Nicaraguan rulers, who found themselves incapable of evading the democratic conditions the plan implied. Their economy was in shambles because of the war, mismanagement, and government corruption. The Nicaraguan population, largely supportive of the Sandinistas for many years, had become increasingly opposed to the government and its repressive, authoritarian security apparatus.

Popular anger, triggered by an endemic economic crisis and a compulsory conscription policy, finally forced the government to acquiesce to the demand of holding elections. Even at the cost of losing power, by 1989 the Sandinistas had realized that the only way to prevent their total political demise was to accept the terms of the Esquipulas Plan, including demands to open the political system and hold free and fair elections.

For the United States, this was a unique opportunity to begin its political offensive in support of democracy in Central America. This offensive openly intruded in Nicaraguan internal affairs and allowed the formation of the National Opposition Union (UNO), a broad coalition of parties and interest groups that would eventually win the 1990 presidential elections.

The triumph of Violeta Chamorro in February 1990 inaugurated a new age in U.S.–Nicaraguan relations. The surprise victory of the UNO candidate, and the decision of the incumbent government to uphold the results of the elections, became a landmark in Latin American history. For the first time a socialist, revolutionary movement exited from office peacefully through electoral means. The irony of an electoral departure of the Sandinistas—following 10 years of U.S.-sponsored military action to bring about the same end—was not lost on many throughout the region.

Deprived of their U.S. backing, the Contras either sought a negotiated solution with the new democratic government or retreated into criminal activities such as kidnapping and extortion. The political spaces brought about by the Esquipulas agreement were finally beginning to pay off. However, even with the end of the Cold War, the momentum of bloody conflict had a logic of its own elsewhere in the region. Often bloody final offensives in El Salvador were clear efforts by the guerrillas to expand negotiating space—even though it was obvious to most that after the 1990 Nicaragua elections, the end of the military crisis in Central America was only a matter of time.

The Invasion of Panama

It was within this auspicious context that U.S. military action in Panama took place.[38] In the early hours of December 20, 1989, U.S. troops invaded Panama. The military operation began after months of unsuccessful negotiations between the Bush Administration, the Panamanian government, and the Latin American countries, mostly within the framework of the OAS. It did not come by surprise.

Throughout the latter part of the 1980s, relations between the United States and Panama had become increasingly strained. Rumors abounded about Panamanian strongman General Manuel Antonio Noriega's nexus with the "narcos." After diligently serving U.S. interests for many decades, Noriega had betrayed his former allies and become one of its most despised adversaries.

No other Central America country has been so decisively influenced by the United States as Panama. The canal, the military bases in the Canal Zone, and the "dollarization" of the economy are the foundations of a relationship unequalled in the Americas. While sometimes strained by differing interests and even political conflicts, these unique bonds had been enduring, longstanding, and strategically useful to both parties.

Panamanian nationalism had receded after the signing of the Panama Canal Treaties (also known as the Torrijos–Carter agreements) in 1977. The mysterious death of General Omar Torrijos two years later triggered a short, yet turbulent, succession within the Panamanian Defense Force, out of which a new leader emerged, Manuel Antonio Noriega. Just as his predecessors, Noriega soon became a trusted and unobtrusive ally of the United States.[39]

During the Central American crisis, Panama played the eclectic wild card, many times adopting positions contrary—yet always short of becoming hostile—to Washington's imposition. Often mired by corruption and deception, the Panamanian leadership had no problems with providing diplomatic and even logistic support to the Sandinista government while profiting from the financial and drug deals that the Contras carried out against the Sandinista government from Panamanian territory. For years, the United States willingly ignored this state of affairs and even tolerated varying degrees of corruption within the defense forces. After all, it was a small price to pay in exchange for using a privileged platform for operations in the area.[40]

American complacency turned into discomfort and finally military action as Noriega's loyalties—and those of his military and civilian cronies—transferred from Washington to the Colombian cartels in the late 1980s. In those days, a common joke making the rounds in Latin America proposed that Noriega's problem was not that he had sold his soul to the Yankees, but rather that he was willing to rent it to almost anybody else. By then, in the twilight of the Cold War and with the fear of communism subsiding rapidly, narco trafficking had been labeled as the United States' top security threat coming from Latin America. Noriega's actions had therefore become unjustifiable and potentially damaging for the White House and the U.S. military and intelligence communities, given the general's blatant disdain for pluralism and democratic values.[41]

Finally, those accumulated tensions, Noriega's arrogant defiance after stealing the 1989 presidential elections from opposition leader Guillermo Endara, the failure of Latin American diplomacy at the OAS through 1989, and the killing of a young American soldier in a road bloc incident triggered "Operation Just Cause." Noriega was toppled after a few hours of combat, but the death toll was much higher than anticipated, and even today the final count of Panamanian casualties is uncertain.

The reaction against the invasion was immediate in Latin America and in the rest of the world. For many countries, the military operations were particularly offensive because they took place as frantic, eleventh hour diplomatic actions were still underway. The OAS negotiations to find a peaceful solution had proven futile, legal considerations not withstanding. Noriega had refused at least two offers to exile himself in Spain or the Dominican Republic, but the United States would not accept any solution short of his resignation as commander in chief of the defense forces and the installation of the winner of the 1988 elections, Guillermo Endara.

Once the military operations in Panama were over, with Noriega prosecuted in the United States on drug-related charges and serious peace negotiations underway in El Salvador and later Guatemala, the attention of the United States shifted to burgeoning conflicts in Europe and the Middle East, where a coalition of military forces led by the United States repelled an Iraqi invasion of Kuwait. This happened as other world affairs took precedence in Washington's foreign policy agenda and as a more peaceful Latin America enjoyed renewed stability resulting from its unprecedented democratic homogeneity.

Against this backdrop, it would be all too tempting to conclude that Central America cannot escape from the historical trends of tension and conflict and alliance and subordination that have characterized its relations with the United States for more than a century. Not only do those tendencies continue to dominate the current debate, but they seem strengthened as the isthmus lags behind the processes of globalization and modernization that characterize the developed world, now haunted by the specter of terrorism just as it was haunted by communism in the past.

The weight of historical factors cannot and should not be overlooked. The asymmetries between Central America and the United States are so overwhelming that it would be very difficult—if all together possible—to imagine scenarios in which the isthmus could overcome the designs of the hegemonic power. This notwithstanding, historical experience also demonstrates that it is not unusual that, in certain historical situations, relative autonomy could be enhanced, and even prevail, over pure geopolitical considerations.

The 1990s allowed Central America more opportunities to prove this point.

CHAPTER 2

Love in Times of Neglect: The 1990s

Introduction

The end of the Cold War ushered in a new period of instability in global affairs. Five decades of strategic stability had ended, and the resulting situation was characterized by disorder and turmoil. Within this context of turbulence, long-standing concerns such as nuclear deterrence and ideological contention were quickly substituted by ethnic, religious, and nationalistic conflicts that had been overshadowed by decades of super-power confrontation. Ancient, fanatical, and often fratricidal wars resurfaced in Central Europe, the Balkans, Western and Central Africa, and Asia Minor. By 1993, the arrival of what President George H. W. Bush called "a new world order" seemed to have degraded into new and more intense levels of global conflict.

This emerging rearrangement of global power and influence brought about unprecedented challenges to U.S. foreign policy. From Brussels to Belgrade and from Belarus to Liberia, American decision-makers were faced with a difficult set of options, neither of which allowed for U.S. isolation. Either dealing with genocide in Bosnia or warlords in Somalia, preventing nuclear escalation between Pakistan and India, or upholding the UN charter in Kuwait, seeking moderation in Iran or the end of the second Intifada in Palestine, the United States was reluctantly becoming the "world policeman" so much dreaded by classical realists and neo-conservatives alike.[1]

The Bush Administration: Adjusting to Pragmatism

It was precisely this global uncertainty that brought about a phase of optimism in hemispheric relations that promised to be different from earlier periods in U.S.–Latin American relations. Framed within an international system increasingly dominated by globalization and democracy, Latin America was portrayed as the U.S. strategic reserve for the twenty-first century—the realm for the dollar's natural expansion locked between the area of the Euro and the area of the Yen.[2]

For Central America, the White House's announcement of its intention to promote an "Enterprise Initiative for the Americas" had more of a symbolic than practical impact. While the Bush-inspired plan to address foreign debt in Latin America provided the region with much-needed relief, the initiative itself promised a new two-way reciprocal trade relation that would surpass the benefits provided by the Caribbean Basin Initiative.

One important, though indirect, outcome of the "Initiative for the Americas" debate in Congress in 1991, was the beginning of an effort to craft a new post–Cold War U.S. agenda toward Central America. Important issues that were obscured by the narrow prism of anticommunism, such as the environment, trade, narcotrafficking and immigration, had been part of the U.S.–Latin American agenda since well before the end of the Cold War. Many of the more substantive discussions on some of these topics took place in the 1970s. In this sense, it is possible to conclude that rather than discovering "new" policy issues, what happened in the early 1990s was a return to a set of earlier issues, some of which were clearly emerging at the highest levels of policy concern.

World trends also became a second decisive factor in the configuration of U.S.–Central America relations throughout the 1990s. The resurgence of environmental issues as a global priority of the United Nations Conference on the Environment and Development (Rio de Janeiro, 1992), the multilateral treatment of the massive migrations brought upon Europe by the fall of the Berlin Wall, the ethnic conflicts in Europe and Africa, and the final negotiations of the Montevideo Rounds of the General Agreement on Tariffs and Trade (GATT) all had a direct regional impact. Even Central America might now begin to focus on issues other than those directly mandated by the United States during the Cold War.

The normalization of the situation in Panama and the electoral defeat of the Sandinistas in Nicaragua marked the gradual dissipation of Central America as a U.S. foreign policy priority. The fall of communism in Europe and the signing of the Peace Agreements in El Salvador (1992) and Guatemala (1996) reinforced this trend.

The United States' positive contribution to the peace accords in Central America in the 1990s, particularly those in El Salvador, is not negligible, however. Without the direct and somewhat forceful intervention of the U.S. Government through the personal involvement of Assistant Secretary of State Bernard Aronson and General Colin Powell, at the time, chairman of the Joint Chiefs of Staff, it is doubtful that the negotiations would have been successful. Indeed, facing the stern opposition of the Salvadoran military, still convinced they could somehow win the war against the FMLN (Farabundo Martí National Liberation Front), the peace negotiations had reached a very dangerous stalemate by mid-1991. Aronson's skillful performance in support of Norwegian-led negotiations, as well as Powell's unequivocal language in conveying to the Salvadoran Armed Forces the Bush Administration's determination to uphold the peace accords, were crucial to breaking the final objections to the plan and resulted in the Oslo agreements.

Similarly, U.S. support was fundamental to ensure the implementation of the peace accords in El Salvador and Guatemala through the direct involvement of the United Nations and the Organization of American States serving as administrators of the agreed terms of disengagement through the in-country establishment of missions (ONUSAL in the case of El Salvador and MINUGUA in Guatemala). While the Central American presidents had made the calling to both organizations as early as 1987, had it not been for U.S. political and financial support, such a positive multilateral presence would have probably suffered considerable shortcomings.

Within this context, the evolution of the U.S.–Central American agenda in the early 1990s is noteworthy. On the one hand, the emphasis moved from confrontation to democratization. For example, this meant supporting transformations in electoral tribunals and in the administration of justice institutions. On the other hand, the lack of an external enemy would soon highlight issues that would bring forth new tensions and even serious conflicts between the United States and its allies in the region.

The early 1990s also witnessed Central America's coming to terms with an aspiration of old: the re-invention of regional integration. Central American integration has been a recurring theme in local politics and economics since the years of independence. Originally associated with military annexation aimed at the preservation (and later reconstitution) of a federal entity resembling that of the United States at the turn of the nineteenth century, it ultimately resulted in the creation of a very imperfect yet effective Central American Common Market in 1959. Successful to the point of becoming a paradigm throughout the 1960s, the Common Market became thwarted by war and violence for three decades, from 1969 to 1990.

By 1991 the Central American countries had agreed to renew the regional integration scheme through the enactment of the Tegucigalpa Protocol, which gave birth to the Central American Integration System (SICA). This new entity included a General Secretariat headquartered in San Salvador, a Central American Parliament (created in 1986 and housed in Guatemala City), a Court of Justice (located in Nicaragua), and a bank (the Central American Integration Bank) with its main offices in Tegucigalpa, Honduras. It was formed by three specialized secretariats (economic, social, and environmental) and 32 integration institutions ranging from a regional transportation council to a confederation of public universities, a disaster agency, and an integration training institute.[3]

The United States welcomed these new trends in regional integration and would eventually take advantage of some of its tenants. Having a more democratic, more united, and harmonious Central America could only serve the larger trade and security interests of the United States, especially at times of muted regional initiatives. This would prove particularly useful in the fight against drug trafficking and, a decade later, in the context of free trade negotiations. Criticisms of SICA notwithstanding, the United States seems to consider Central American integration a desirable scenario for the twenty-first century.[4]

Benign Neglect

The advent of a Democratic administration in the White House in 1993 did little to raise the overall profile of Latin America in Washington. Warren Christopher's appointment as Secretary of State underlined the administration's commitment to Washington's traditional geopolitical priorities: the North Atlantic alliance and the Middle East.

U.S. foreign policy decision-makers found themselves in a period of growing isolationism, a recurring characteristic of U.S. foreign policy. Caught by surprise by the fall of the socialist world, the United States found itself lacking a cohesive doctrine that could fill the voids left behind by the end of the Cold War.[5] Even with the success of the United States' first formal military intervention in the Middle East (the invasion of Kuwait and Iraq), President Bush's attempt to invent a "new world order" was rejected in the United States as overly ambitious.

President Clinton was elected because of his attention to domestic issues—specifically the economy and employment generation. With little prior experience in foreign affairs, the president initially stayed in his policy comfort zone, leaving little time for Latin American affairs. One of the products of this doctrinal vacuum was the abandonment of any comprehensive focus on Latin America. The exception to this rule was, of course,

Mexico. Indeed, the major hemispheric concerns for the United States during this period revolved around three events that became pivotal in Mexico's contemporary history: the growing movement in Mexico to align with the United States and Canada through the North American Free Trade Agreement, ratified by the three countries in late 1993; the violent eruption of an indigenous insurrection in Chiapas, led by the Zapatista National Liberation Front and its Hollywood-esque leader, Subcomandante Marcos in late 1994;[6] and the huge financial crisis that put Mexico on the verge of bankruptcy, thus triggering the so-called Tequila effect throughout Latin America in early 1995.

It was in the context of the drift of U.S. foreign policy during this period that the negative agenda for Latin America emerged. This agenda would guarantee collisions on a variety of issues and would come to dominate U.S.–Latin American relations for the balance of the decade.

An Age of Decreasing Expectations[7]

The United States' lack of interest in Central America in the 1990s intensified as the decade progressed. Overnight, the region disappeared from the front pages of most U.S. newspapers and from the nightly news. Simultaneously, other extra-regional as well as nonhemispheric actors appeared in the region. This process had begun years before, as a reaction to a potentially explosive situation that threatened to expand the war in Central America well beyond its geographical boundaries. The novelty was that these extra-regional actors were called in by the Central American governments as new partners for development.[8]

The resources of these new actors were significant, particularly in the face of the downward spiral in U.S. aid with the collapse of the Soviet Union. After 1992 the European Union and Taiwan displaced the United States as the most important donor in the region. While it would be difficult to establish a direct relationship between the reduction of aid and a parallel loss of U.S. political influence in Central America, undoubtedly the decreasing levels of cooperation meant bigger margins of autonomy for the countries in the region.

There are some notable examples to this regard. From 1994 to 1998, Central America established preferential associations at the highest level with Mexico, Chile, and Canada. In an unprecedented demonstration of interest, the Prime Minister of Japan met with the Presidents of Central America in San Jose, Costa Rica, in August 1995. His visit was followed by those of Presidents Hertzog (Germany), Kim (South Korea), and Menem (Argentina), all of whom held regional summits with their Central American counterparts. Even Foreign Minister Evgueni Primakov, soon to become Primer Minister of the Russian Federation, met with his Central American colleagues in San Jose in September 1997.

These meetings would have been inconsequential had it not been that all of them—except Primakov's—took place months and even years before President Clinton decided to visit Central America. Symbolism aside, the cooperation agreements reached and the financial and technical commitments made during those encounters in the absence of a well-defined U.S. policy were welcomed in the region. The Monroe Doctrine had clearly lost its original meaning.

The profile of a relationship based on negative issues (the so-called negative agenda) between Central America and the United States became noticeable in the early 1990s.[9] Disagreements centered around seven issues: immigration, textiles, drugs, trade (especially pertaining to nontariff barriers), expropriations, car theft, and intellectual property rights, all considered to be threats to U.S. interests.

It would be difficult to imagine a more complex and conflicting set of matters and, not surprisingly, the impact they would have in the bilateral relations. While not new, the issues at hand had been systematically ignored during the years of the Cold War in the context of great power rivalry and the U.S. desire to preserve the edge in geopolitical competition against the Soviet Union. Probably the most vicious but lesser known of them all was drug trafficking. Indeed, as the Tower Commission and other independent sources demonstrated, during the 1980s the CIA had knowledge of narco activities that were carried out by organizations that supported or carried-out counterrevolutionary activities in Nicaragua. Manuel Noriega, the strongman of Panama, was one of the most notable examples of this.[10]

With the Cold War passing into history, the resurgence of the negative agenda was inevitable. President Clinton had a limited interest in foreign policy and was distracted by other matters. His secretary of state all but discounted the region entirely.[11] Thus, the primary actors in foreign policy, particularly with regard to Latin America, were the foreign affairs bureaucrats, elected officials, and their staffers in the U.S. Congress. Emphasizing job creation and economic development, the Clinton administration prioritized domestic concerns and paid particular attention to private business grievances about the abuses supposedly committed by foreign agents against U.S. interests offshore. While weak by themselves, these private concerns had a foothold in Congress, where special interest groups and major campaign contributors made a powerful lobby against so-called anti-American behavior.

Hence, Guatemala, Honduras, and El Salvador were soon accused of child labor exploitation in the textile industries. In this case the scandal involved conflicting business and regional interests among three U.S. enterprises: Fruit of the Loom, Sarah Lee, and Hanes. Costa Rica and Nicaragua were put on the spot regarding property rights and service contracts in which large Democratic or Republican contributors were involved. Belize was accused by Texas-based interests of not taking a stronger stand against car thefts that supposedly affected up to 25% of Belize's cars.

The denunciations also involved intellectual property rights violations (Honduras, Nicaragua, and El Salvador), drug trafficking and money laundering activities (Panama and Guatemala), and disloyal competition and dumping practices in agriculture (Costa Rica, Honduras, and Colombia) and their banana quota agreement with the European Union against the interests of U.S. transnationals Dole and Chiquita Brands.[12]

The close bonds between the U.S. Government and private business interests are not appreciated abroad. Neither is the latter's capacity to influence foreign policy decisions above and beyond the national interest. These long-standing traits of U.S. politics had a double negative impact on U.S.–Central American relations. First, they undermined Washington's credibility and leadership in the region. Indeed, Central American governments complained bitterly about what they considered to be the capitulation of the executive branch before private interests' attempts to make money—at the expense of Central America's poor and dispossessed.

Worse still, the denunciations ended up affecting the image of the United States as a preponderant regional actor. The World Trade Organization and even U.S. federal courts rejected most U.S. complaints against Central American practices, providing Costa Rica and Guatemala with consequential legal victories in the cases of textiles and agricultural goods.[13]

Ultimately, the negative agenda was subdued as a result of initiatives taken by Central American leaders themselves in the mid-1990s. Yet it is a continuing theme in U.S.–Central American relations.

The Alliance for Sustainable Development

In late 1993 the Central American Presidents met in Richmond, Virginia, with the Association of Southern Governors. Convened by the Governor of Puerto Rico, Pedro Roselló, the meeting was proof of the new conditions that made the Greater Caribbean an area of geopolitical and economic interest of the Southern United States. For Central America, the meeting was a good opportunity to bypass a neglectful Clinton Administration and a unique regional approach to explore creative alternatives to a Washington-led relationship. It also symbolized the growing activism of state governments in the United States in foreign affairs decision-making, particularly directed at expanding the commercial relations between their local jurisdictions and other countries.

While the meeting itself accomplished little and would not be repeated for five years, the trip of the Central American presidents to Richmond had two positive outcomes. The first one was symbolic: it highlighted a new creativity within Central America to establish close ties with leaders of an important region of the United States independent of the federal government. The second one was practical: it forced the White House to avoid a diplomatic blunder, for the visiting Central American dignitaries were invited at the last moment of their stay to a working meeting with President Clinton. However, aside from a meaningless joint statement, little was accomplished at this gathering.

At that meeting Guatemalan President Ramiro de Leon presented President Clinton with the idea of forging a formal U.S.–Central American "alliance for sustainable development." This alliance was meant to be a U.S.–Central American preferential association whose principal objective would be to promote regional development, democracy, and the preservation of the environment. President Clinton's reaction to the Central American proposal was courteous but noncommittal—so much so that the initiative was not even mentioned by the media.

Almost a year later, in August 1994, the Central American presidents met again, this time in their fourteenth summit, in Guacimo, Costa Rica. By then, three new presidents had been elected (Costa Rica's José María Figueres, El Salvador's Armando Calderon Sol, and Panama's Ernesto Perez Balladares), and two others (Guatemala's Ramiro de Leon and Nicaragua's Violeta Chamorro) would soon leave office.

The Guacimo meeting became a landmark in Central American history because at the initiative of Costa Rican President Figueres, the leaders decided to transform Ramiro de Leon's unsuccessful proposal to Bill Clinton into an alliance with the rest of the world. Based on the principles of the United Nations Conference on the Environment and Development (UNCED, Rio de Janeiro, 1992), the Central American Alliance for Sustainable Development (ALIDES) became the last and most important phase of a regional integration initiative dating from 1991. The document was signed at the environmental summit held near the active volcano at Masaya, Nicaragua, in October 1994.

ALIDES represented a departure point for Central America in at least three ways. First, it demonstrated a paradigm transformation in the regional definition of development. Policy-makers had become aware of the need to incorporate social, political, and environmental factors to a concept that for decades was exclusively determined by economic growth variables. Second, it underlined the democratic nature of the governments of Central America. Nowhere before in the history of Central America had fully democratic governments signed such an overarching agreement. Last, it signaled the advent of a serious attempt by the regional partners to present their own priorities to the international donor community.[14]

Likewise, in Guacimo the Presidents demonstrated a growing concern about being left out of the emerging North American trade bloc. As a result, they called upon the United States for parity with NAFTA and they agreed to undertake all future trade negotiations as a joint endeavor, a bold and unprecedented initiative that was bitterly contested by commercial elites in Costa Rica and Panama.

The Joint Declaration Central America–USA[15]

Parallel to the December 1994 Summit of the Americas in Miami, which called for free trade throughout the Americas by 2005, the U.S. and Central American heads of state signed a joint declaration—the Central American–United States of America Joint Declaration (CONCA–USA)—to promote environmental cooperation and sustainability. This agreement, renewed and expanded in 2001, has served as a model agreement to foster shared U.S.–Central American goals in the region.

Even when the final text of CONCA–USA turned out to be not as integral as Central America expected, it was significant for several reasons. First, it was the only document other than the Miami Declaration that was signed during the Summit of the Americas. This provided Central America with an important symbolic victory *vis-à-vis* other regions of the hemisphere. Second, it represented the first agreement ever signed by Central America's civilian elected presidents as a regional bloc with the United States—unprecedented in the history of the region. CONCA–USA was also important because it set the stage of President Clinton's first visit to Central America (San Jose, Costa Rica, on May 7–9, 1997).

Clinton and Hurricane Mitch

The Caribbean Basin area has endured countless natural disasters throughout the twentieth century. No doubt, the most destructive on record during this period was Hurricane Mitch. The 180-mile-hour hurricane was downgraded to a tropical depression by the time it stalled on October 29, 1998, over Honduras. It hovered there for 72 hours, dumping countless millions of gallons of rain throughout the isthmus (except Costa Rica and Panama). It caused catastrophic flooding and mudslides in Nicaragua and Honduras and severely impacted El Salvador and Guatemala. As a result of this tragedy, some 11,000 people died and billions of dollars were lost.

Figure 2.1 Satellite image of Hurricane Mitch.

From a purely economic point of view, Mitch made Nicaragua and Honduras retreat several decades in their development (Figure 2.1).[16]

The U.S. response to the tragedy was immediate and generous. Even when the administration lessened its initial interest in Central America as the devastation slipped into media oblivion, the policy toward the region in the wake of the hurricane, and its implementation, was exemplary.

Only two weeks after the hurricane struck Central America, in November 1998, President Clinton requested the private visit of former President George Bush to assess the damages in Honduras on his behalf.[17]

By December 11, 1998, when the Central American presidents convened with President Clinton in Washington, the administration had already decided to allocate up to $300 million in emergency aid for the region, including $150 million from the Pentagon, $87 million from USAID, and $63 million from the Department of Agriculture.[18]

On that occasion, President Clinton also announced the administration's decision to suspend the deportations of Honduran and Nicaraguan nationals from the United States until January 31, 1999. The extension was subsequently further extended. Ardently debated throughout the mid- and late-1990s in both Central America and the United States, immigration is one of those hot-button intermestic issues for which no definitive resolution is in sight. The Nicaraguan Adjustment and Central American Relief Act (NACARA) passed in late 1997 was intended to provide immigration benefits and relief from deportation for select Central Americans during this period. However, it is clear that the legislation did little to allay suspicions about deportations of Central American nationals.

During this period, in one Congressional hearing after another, U.S. diplomats, elected officials, and specialists hotly debated the pros and cons of deportations of thousands of Central Americans who were in the United States without documentation. One U.S. congressman openly stated that "... if our government goes hog wild and tries to send a whole bunch of people back, we are going to have to shut down our business because we have not got the people ... the fact that the economy of our country depends to a very large extent on the two or three million Hispanics that have come here just lately, and all you have got to do is look at every hotel around the city of Washington, just about every restaurant and I think what they have done is they have filled in...."[19] This suspension was again extended until March 1999.[20]

Finally, during his high-profile second visit to Central America (Posoltega, Nicaragua) in March of 1999, President Clinton announced his government's decision to request from Congress the allocation of nearly $700 million in special funding for the countries most affected by Mitch. If approved, this contribution would make the United States and the European Union the largest donors in the region.[21]

From a public policy-making point of view, the administration's response was also positive. Indeed, by late January 1999 the president had already convened a task force spearheaded by the State Department and USAID. This group was responsible for the total coordination of the U.S. government's actions in Central America.

In briefing the press corps, Secretary of State Counselor and task force Coordinator Wendy Sherman summarized U.S. goals in dealing with Central America:[22] support for democratic stability, the revitalization of national economies, the prevention of mass migration to the United States, and attention to the environmental degradation caused in part by Hurricane Mitch.

It is significant that U.S. policymakers were able to transcend the short-term humanitarian perspective. The need to truly transform Central America by inducing its governments to deal with the social and economic vulnerabilities on a long-term basis was finally acknowledged. The United States also decided to funnel as many resources as possible through local and communal organizations—municipalities included—to enhance their impact and reduce the sources of potential corruption, a problem that is endemic in Central American governance.[23]

The administration's high-profile management of the crisis in Central America was also noteworthy. President Clinton's announced visit to the region was delayed as a result of the impeachment proceedings. Nevertheless, his meeting with his Central American colleagues in Washington, DC, as well as the early fact-finding missions undertaken by former President George H. W. Bush, First Lady Hilary Rodham-Clinton, and Tipper Gore, the wife of Vice President Gore, were powerful, albeit temporary, indications of the region's preferential status. During the 1990s, no other country or region of Latin America had been visited so frequently by a sitting U.S. president, even in times of extraordinary calamity.

This newly positive scenario was soon to be obscured by the historical limits to Central American prominence in the U.S. foreign policy agenda.

First, the resources for humanitarian relief and reconstruction committed by the administration did not necessarily come from "fresh" budget sources. Rather, they were funds that had already been allocated for other purposes in the countries most affected by Mitch. In this case the administration expedited the appropriation mechanism to facilitate the disbursement procedures. When new resources were needed, as in the case of the $700 million requested from Congress, the administration was immediately drawn into a testy partisan quagmire with the Republican majority.[24]

It is relevant in this regard to use the "lame duck" metaphor that affected the second Reagan and Clinton administrations to illustrate the likelihood of Central America becoming the hostage of U.S. internal politics. In both cases a weak but determined White House was deterred from greater support for Central America by a strong and partisan Congress, which was increasingly hostile to any Clinton-led initiatives because of the impeachment proceedings related to his White House affair with Monica Lewinsky. In both instances the White House lost its bid and could only save face after making painful concessions to the lawmakers.

In the case of the Central American post-Mitch package, the Republican majority was able to trap the White House in the web of interested politics. First, the lawmakers demanded the inclusion of Africa and U.S. farmers and steelworkers as recipients of the special funds requested by the executive. This inclusion meant an increase of the original $700 million to $1.9 billion. Second, Congress refused to allocate new resources for those purposes but rather wanted the president to choose between them or keeping some of his most-cherished domestic social investments in health care and education. The president was able to avoid this embarrassing course of action by threatening to veto the proposed legislation. Yet, in the final analysis, the resources were only approved as a part of the deals brokered over the funding of the air campaign in Kosovo, and then only in a much lesser amount than originally requested by the White House.

As the urgency over Mitch's destruction dissipated, so did the administration's capacity to impose its will over the particular agendas of the government's specialized bureaucracies. One case in point had to do with the most important measure to help Central America's long-term recovery: the enhancement of trade preferences for its products in U.S. markets. This possibility was strongly opposed and flatly rejected by the United States Trade Representative (USTR) office.[25] The measure also generated many ill feelings among the Central American presidents.[26]

Similarly, the U.S.Immigration and Naturalization Service (INS) only reluctantly accepted President Clinton's temporary suspension of deportations in January 1999. By early February 1999, the INS already had begun deportations of Central Americans to their countries of origin. This practice was only temporarily deterred on the eve of President Clinton's trip to Central America, and even then, the President acknowledged his legal incapacity to do anything about it. The reaction of the Central American leaders to what they considered an outrageous demonstration of inhumanity was ironic. They blamed the United States for being partially responsible for the Central American exodus resulting from the regional crisis in the 1980s[27]—one of the many negative unintended consequences of the Cold War approach that the United States had taken to the region.

Even with enhanced activism to deal with Mitch on the part of Central America's leadership, the manner by which the Central American countries handled the Mitch tragedy was insufficient at best and irresponsible at worse. The regional governments were slow and indecisive in supporting the White House before Congress. They could not develop a common approach to soliciting reconstruction funds, they had no common strategy, and they failed to develop a serious lobby to represent their interests in the halls of Congress, where so many critical decisions are made.[28] This situation only reinforced the difficulties that Central America has had, and continues to have, in its quest for a higher profile and priority in the U.S. foreign policy agenda, even in the most critical moments of its history.

A New President Bush

The contested election of George W. Bush in November 2000 heralded the arrival of a new brand of Republican conservatism that resembled the views of the ideological cold warriors of the 1980s, more than those of the pragmatic patricians who had succeeded President Reagan a decade before.

Indeed, while the young Bush had campaigned under the premise of "compassionate conservatism" to lure the centrist rank and file of his party, it soon became clear that his administration would not honor that commitment. This became apparent as the born-again president favored the counsel and political activism of the religious right and called upon many of President Reagan's foreign policy experts (notably those who had been involved in the murky Central American scenario of the 1980s). He quickly abandoned Clinton and Gore's liberal internationalism, substituting it with a strident criticism of multilateral institutions, the United Nations in particular.

President Bush's foreign policy positions reflected the views and priorities that had been long cherished by the benefactors of the so-called Project for A New American Century. This group, formed in the early 1990s by distinguished and well-known Republican ideologues, had followed the lead of the Reagan era's Santa Fe Group and had set the new president's international agenda well before the election had taken place.[29]

In Latin America President Bush's election generated hopes for an enhanced hemispheric profile in U.S. foreign policy. After all, Mr. Bush—a former Texan governor who had been sensitive to his immediate neighbors in Mexico and whose brother was the governor of Florida and spoke Spanish—had pledged to "treat Latin America with dignity" and "to provide renewed attention to the region, and to link its future to the future of the US." He had also stated that he would "look south not as an afterthought, but as a fundamental commitment of (his) presidency."[30]

Similarly, Bush's position on free trade had received praise from the Latin American business community, whose high hopes on the matter had been dampened by President's Clinton insincere efforts to get "fast track" authority from Congress during his White House tenure. Indeed, following a long-standing Republican position, the Bush administration had voiced its strong support to free trade and deregulation in the hemisphere and beyond, a vision he seemed willing to pursue with as much determination as he had pledged to combat what he offhandedly called Latin America's "export problems": environmental trouble, illegal immigration, crime, drugs, and violence. The president had been blunt and direct on this issue: in Latin America, he said, "… we seek not just good neighbors, but good partners, not just progress, but shared prosperity."

Electoral high hopes regarding Latin America, however, quickly deteriorated into a focus on Mexico and seemed to be bogged down in traditional Eurocentric concerns and a disdain for nation-building that characterized the preceding administration. Any hopes for a different approach to Latin America however, were dashed by the unexpected and devastating blows of terrorists against the World Trade Center in New York and the Pentagon in Washington. The September 2001 surprise "completely changed the nation's focus."[31] The attacks of 9-11 and the subsequent military actions in Afghanistan (2001–2002) and Iraq (2003) produced a compelling new rationale and approach for U.S. foreign policy in general and U.S.–Latin American relations in particular. With regard to Central America, these events have generated a shifting of the regional security priorities from the seemingly inconsequential negative agenda of the 1990s to a reconstituted hegemonic strategy that would center upon terrorism and its global ramifications.

CHAPTER 3

Foreign Policy Dilemmas in the Post–Cold War Era: New Challenges, Old Responses?

Introduction

Even as a new post–Cold War framework of relations is being established between the United States and Central America that pivots around security issues defined by the threat of terrorism, other critical issues remain on the U.S.–Central America agenda that must be addressed if the region is to meet the expectations and demands of its growing population.

Many of these issues reflect a broader hemispheric consensus over policy and have been subjects of local debate in the region for decades, both during and after the Cold War. In the era of globalization, they tend to be intermestic in nature; coalitions of interests are formed utilizing advanced communication (Internet, wireless communication, blogs) within the respective countries, in neighboring countries, or with governmental and nongovernmental organizations in and out of the region.

These issues may have taken on greater urgency in the more open policy environment period of the 1990s, coincident with the deepening of democracy in the region. However, in the post–9-11 world, their salience is diminished because of the new animating concept of U.S. foreign policy focusing on security and antiterrorism. Just as the black-and-white challenge of Soviet domination was used to justify U.S. predominance in the Cold War era, so the black-and-white threat of global terrorism has been used to justify a new assertiveness in U.S. foreign policy in the post–9-11 era. The return to a monochromatic understanding of global affairs, known in some circles as "blunt unilateralism," complicates the search for solutions to a range of everyday concerns in the region that must be addressed if Central American well-being is to improve.[1]

A second, equally important, factor accompanies this peculiar understanding of world and regional priorities. President Bush and his administration's most senior policy-makers (as well as many Democrats who held positions of leadership under Clinton) believe in the infinite capacity of the free market to generate liberty, prosperity, and democratic governance if left alone to work its way around.

Their mantra is unequivocal. In the words of U.S. Deputy Assistant Secretary of State for Western Hemisphere Affairs, Roger F. Noriega, free trade agreements and other U.S. efforts to open markets and remove barriers to entrepreneurship "will transform societies by allowing countries to market their comparative advantages and domestic resources, and to attract investment from abroad. They will encourage good governance, because few will invest in places where corruption is rampant and the rule of law is weak. Trade accords also advance sound workers' rights and better environmental standards."

Furthermore, he said, "Poverty will disappear only when individuals are granted the opportunity to unleash their creative genius and profit from their labor. We are urging our partners, therefore, to remove impediments to business creation, improve access to capital, strengthen property rights, and revise their labor laws."[2]

This dogmatic understanding of democratic development as a byproduct of market economics constitutes a problematic point of departure when addressing highly underdeveloped countries such as those in Central America. It is ideologically consistent with globalization and neo-liberal propositions and is solidly entrenched in the policy directives of all the international financial organizations. However, it tends to disregard the importance of politics as an independent variable whose complexity in terms of power relations goes well beyond the limited interactions that occur among economic actors within the narrow boundaries of the marketplace.

Furthermore, it highlights the logic and motivations behind the reluctance and mistrust with which neo-conservatives (or "neo-liberals," as they are called in the Latin American and European political tradition) approach the integral agendas favored by more comprehensive development models. These models favor distribution strategies built upon publicly funded, welfare safety networks conducted within strongly regulated regimes.

There are indeed gray areas between dogmatic, free-market-driven ideologues and heart-bleeding apologies for the state. Yet the history of Central America shows that seldom have these areas been predominant in the region. The sole exception is Costa Rica, the oldest and, until recently, the most stable of the isthmian republics. Moreover, in the broader context of its relations with the United States, it is safe to conclude that in a more polarized context than the present one, the likelihood of reform-oriented policies in Central America looks dim. This only underscores the need to bring the other issues into perspective, and to reiterate their relevance even at a time when color blindness seems to have settled in for a long stay.

Security: Old and New Priorities

The end of the regional crisis in Central America in the late 1980s brought about a significant change in the United States' security perceptions of the area.[3] In the years of the Cold War, the United States was fundamentally preoccupied with communist aggression. In the 1990s the United States defined international crime, drug trafficking, illegal immigration, weapons smuggling, and car theft, in particular, as the new security threats to its national interests.[4]

The Pentagon's decision to move the headquarters of the U.S. Southern Command (SOUTHCOM) from Panama to Miami, the suspension of military aid to the Central American armed forces, and the strong public support of the United States to the new roles of the armies in a democratic society, were all indicators of the profound changes experienced by the relationship during that decade.[5]

Such extraordinary transformation notwithstanding, the security agenda continued to complicate the U.S.–Central America relationship even in a significantly different international context. In defining drug trafficking as a "war," the United States favored the involvement of the Central American armed forces in narcotics interdiction and intelligence-gathering activities. While resisted in other regions of Latin America, this renewed presence of the military in Central American public life, which had been severely reduced as part of the peace negotiations, had two negative consequences. First, it undermined the efforts to strengthen the civilian police's effectiveness and professionalism amidst generalized societal critiques regarding its honesty and overall capacity to neutralize the increasing wave of violent crime. Second, it opened the way for military officers and their institutions to regain their lost prestige and political clout. This was an unwelcome development, given the role the military had traditionally played in recent Central American history.[6]

In short, far from keeping the soldiers in their barracks, the overarching roles and missions attributed to the armed forces in the presumably newly democratized societies of Central America ended in militarizing the still ill-defined national development agendas.

This trend was further stimulated by the appearance of new, more comprehensive concepts of security, invented by civilian scholars that widened its definition from strictly defense-related issues to almost everything encompassed in the notion of "human development," newly crafted by the United Nations. Indeed, the 1990s witnessed the arrival of a new generation of concepts including "human security" (a byproduct of "human development"), South America's "cooperative security," Central America's "democratic security," and the so-called strategies of integral security or multidimensional security, as adopted by the OAS in 2003.[7]

Hence, by 1996 the Central American armies were performing a wide array of nontraditional duties including the protection of the environment, the construction of schools, roads and hospitals, the provision of medical services, and the support of police contingents in dealing with urban crime.[8]

It is inevitable that one would ponder the significance of these decisions in the aftermath of the terrorist attacks on September 11. Only a few days after those tragic events occurred, the Central American presidents met at the agricultural school of *El Zamorano* in Honduras to voice their solidarity and support to the U.S. government and the American people. Their joint declaration, the Zamorano Declaration, though, went beyond moral support to include measures to curb potential terrorism activities in the isthmus and to strengthen the operational capabilities of their security forces, including the military.

The United States responded quickly to the call of the Central American leaders. In January 2002 the U.S. Department of Defense announced the beginning of its new cooperative effort with the Central American armed forces. After a decade of significant disengagement, the Pentagon declared its intention to reestablish operational as well as logistic linkages with its Central American counterparts. Salient among these were funds to enhance outdated equipment (including helicopters and patrol boats) and new training programs in the United States. These actions included the Nicaraguan Armed Forces, an institution with which the United States had little official contact since the fall of Nicaragua's dictatorial President Anastasio Somoza in 1979.

By 2002 the Central American security agenda had been transformed. The former concerns regarding international crime, drug trafficking, illegal immigration, weapons smuggling, and car theft were now secondary issues with regard to fighting terrorism and its potential agents. Central America was by no means a major area of serious U.S. concern (mostly focused on the so-called Triple Frontier between Brazil, Argentina, and Paraguay), but the policy priority was hemispheric and the isthmus was rapidly incorporated into Washington's geopolitical considerations.[9]

Table 3.1 Foreign Military Financing for Central America (thousands of U.S. dollars)[a]

	Costa Rica	El Salvador	Guatemala	Honduras	Nicaragua	Panama
1999	0	43	0	116	0	595
2000	0	104	0	5	0	0
2001	0	0	0	0	0	0
2002	0	1000	0	0	500	0
2003	0	2400	0	168	1000	990
2004	0	5000	0	2375	938	2000
2005 estimate	0	1400	500	992	496	900

[a]*The Foreign Military Financing (FMF) program offers grants and loans to help countries buy U.S.-produced weapons, defense equipment, defense services, and military training. FMF serves to fund arms transfers. Military training is provided through the International Military Education and Training Program (IMET). Some FMF is used for training, however. See http://ciponline.org/facts/fmf.htm#FMFas and http://www.ciponline.org/facts/imet.htm.*

Source: http://ciponline.org/facts/fmf.htm#FMFas

Though the United States had consistently supported counter-narcotics initiatives since the days of the Reagan Administration, the fight against terrorism quickly became preeminent. It allowed for a whole new effort, the first serious one in more than 20 years, to upgrade, renew, and enhance the training, logistical, intelligence, and operational capabilities of the Central American armed forces. It also called for the improvement of military hardware, much of which had become obsolete even before the end of the region's political and military crisis in the 1980s. The end result was the most important increase of U.S. military cooperation with Central America in the past 20 years (Tables 3.1 and 3.2).

The new global outlook adopted by the United States after 9-11 also revived the logic of submission on the part of Central America. This was particularly true once U.S. military operations broke out in Afghanistan and later in Iraq. Indeed, in both cases, all the Central American countries were quick to adhere to Washington's positions. Furthermore, in the case of Iraq, three Central American countries—El Salvador, Honduras, and Nicaragua—sent military and medical personnel to the theater of operations under Spanish command. Three others—Guatemala, Panama, and Costa Rica—became part of the Coalition of the Willing, a cornerstone of the White House's strategy to neutralize charges that it was isolated from world public opinion in the occupation of Iraq.[10] By 2005, however, only El Salvador maintained its troops in Iraq, a strategic decision that has

Table 3.2 International Military Education and Training for Central America (thousands of U.S. dollars/students trained)

	Costa Rica	El Salvador	Guatemala	Honduras	Nicaragua	Panama
1999	240/53	491/181	253/103	560/221	200/5	0
2000	280/69	523/143	228/19	548/208	5	117/12
2001	297/51	653/243	291/33	546/111	194/135	131/17
2002	389/66	814/354	350/78	655/208	372/61	178/23
2003	336/46	1160/274	350/89	724/222	600/104	209/31
2004	0/0	1400/389	504/174	1300/319	779/91	558/34
2005 estimate	0/0	1600/421	350/104	1100/268	600/70	600/37
2006 request	50/2	1600/421	400/139	1100/268	600/70	600/37

Source: http://www.state.gov/m/rm/rls/cbj/

allowed this country to become the staunchest, most reliable, and publicly acknowledged ally of the United States in Central America.

Therefore, by late 2003, the Central American countries were fully incorporated into the U.S.-led war against terrorism. They participated in virtually all hemispheric initiatives regarding security. This meant joining the Declaration on Security in the Americas, the Inter-American Convention Against Terrorism, the Declaration of Montevideo on border and financial controls, and the inter-American strategy to combat threats to cyber security. Central American representatives also participated in the Miami experts' meeting on Confidence and Security Building Measures. High-level officials, including the presidents and foreign and defense ministers, began a very intense epoch of regional and bilateral visits to the United States to meet with U.S. foreign policy decision-makers, including President Bush, Defense Secretary Donald Rumsfeld, and Secretary of State Colin Powell.

Similarly, the Central American Armed Forces Conference (CFAC), the regional council of the military commanders of Guatemala, El Salvador, Honduras, and Nicaragua created in 1997, was reinvigorated. For years, this organization had been mostly devoted to the mitigation of natural disasters, yet this time it was convened by the presidents to coordinate all regional efforts aimed at curtailing the terrorist threat. The CFAC intervention in matters other than humanitarian relief in times of natural disasters took hold on December 13, 2002. On that date the CFAC released its CFAC Plan of Integral Cooperation against Terrorism, Organized Crime, and their Related Activities. This plan was presented and approved by the Central American presidents in 2003 and became the backbone of the new security framework in the region.

During the summit of Tegucigalpa (June 29–30, 2005) the Central American presidents finally accepted the CFAC proposal to create a regional fast-deployment military task force whose main objective would be to fight terrorism, organized crime, and their related activities. The presidential decision was significant for Central America in that it ended the short-lived but formal effort to separate public security from national defense that was codified through the Treaty of Central American Democratic Security of 1995.[11]

Even in times of democratic governance in Central America, this development, which occurred in a larger international context of blunt unilateralism, brought back the armed forces as major players in regional politics. This role, which Central American militaries had never neglected but which was obscured amidst the post-war negotiations that strengthened civil leadership and institutions, continues to highlight the incomplete nature of Central American democratic transition. It also brings about a renewed concern as to the likelihood of undue military involvement in public life, very much in the same way this occurred during the years of the Cold War regarding presumed communist activism.

Meetings were called more frequently to prepare regional contingency plans against the newly found enemy, and joint regional military maneuvers commenced in May 2004. Compared to other moments, however, this time the armed forces of Central America were not simulating operations to ease the human suffering caused by the impact of a potentially devastating natural disaster, nor were they raiding presumed drug-carrying vessels in the sea. Rather, they were preparing to neutralize a terrorist attack under the close scrutiny of U.S. Special Forces.

Several joint exercises with U.S. military contingents carrying out "civic action" style operations resumed. Military maneuvers were held in Honduras and El Salvador (New Horizons, 2004/2005), Guatemala (Maya Jaguar Plan, 2004) and Guatemala, Belize, Honduras and Nicaragua (Operation Round-up, 2005). Central American troops also participated in the Department of Defense's hemispheric exercise, Commando Forces 2004. They continue to consider the possibility of joining Chile and Brazil in their military duties in Haiti in compliance with, and under the mandate of, the Organization of American States General Assembly.

It is also noteworthy that all Central American countries but Costa Rica have supported the U.S. demand to prevent its military personnel from being subject to the jurisdiction of the International Criminal Court. This is further proof of the importance attributed to U.S. military collaboration by the Central American nations. It is also a clear indication of the region's unwillingness to upset its powerful neighbor even at the cost of constricting the duties of a major multilateral agency originally empowered with the support of the Clinton Administration to address war crimes and genocide in Central Europe and Africa.

The question remains whether this renewed emphasis on military collaboration with—and strategic submission to—the United States will produce undue tensions and even serious breaches in the still vulnerable, weak, and doubtfully institutionalized Central American democratic systems. It is no secret that during the Cold War, U.S. concerns over the spread of communism led to some of the most horrifying human rights abuses in Central America. At the time, the region was dominated by the military, which had little respect for the rule of law. While the situation has improved since then, even democratically elected governments could unwillingly end up fostering questionable practices under the notion of "preventive war" or the need to uphold "homeland security." For evidence of this possibility, one need look no further than the Patriot Act. Promulgated by the U.S. Congress in response to 9-11, it includes numerous elements that are seriously questioned by legal critics and civil libertarians alike.[12]

One of the fears of the growing "security-zation" of the Central American national agendas and of the isthmus' relationship with the United States is that it could result in the region reenacting some of the most perverse political cycles of its recent past. Indeed, in a region still dominated by weak political parties and extremely unpopular state institutions, authoritarian tendencies are still pervasive and could easily become dominant in contexts of extreme poverty and growing social discontent. Venezuela and the Andean Region are ominous examples in this regard.

In all likelihood, the United States will continue to exert significant pressures upon the Central American governments to improve their security performance. Not all its pressures will be aimed at enlarging the region's military establishment, though. In an effort to thwart some countries' insistent requests to expand their armaments, high-level Bush Administration officials warned the Central American governments in 2003 and 2004 that a regional balance of power was desirable.

These warnings accompanied a bitter dispute between Nicaragua and the United States over 2000 Soviet-made surface-to–air portable missiles (SAM-7) in the custody of the Nicaraguan Armed Forces from the war years in the 1980s. Fearful that the missiles could end up in the black market, the United States demanded their destruction. While 366 missiles where indeed destroyed under presidential authority in late 2004, domestic feuds between the executive and the legislative branches inhibited the continuation of the task, generating a serious confrontation between Managua and

Washington. This incident clearly illustrates the limits of both countries' willingness to concede on matters pertaining to their perceived objectives of national security.

The early twenty-first century has witnessed the reconstitution of U.S. hegemony over Central America. This has been the result of several factors, most notably the impact of the 9-11 attacks on U.S. national security strategy and the ensuing Bush Administration's war on terrorism. This trend is historically consistent with the pattern of intervention and neglect that has dominated U.S.–Central American relations since 1898. It is to be expected that the current phase will continue as long as the international circumstances demand or until the domestic consensus within the U.S. government allows. Sooner or later, the cycle will resume its inevitable evolution.

Nevertheless, it is still unclear whether a second Bush Administration will be able to view Central America beyond the narrow confines of its security-led perspective. Even some of the president's stauncher and more conservative allies acknowledge the existence of social and economic issues whose resolution is crucial for Central American long-term stability. Dealing with those issues and putting the U.S. behind the necessary national and regional efforts to achieve a lasting solution to them would be a fundamental step toward a new understanding of U.S. and Central American common challenges in a very uncertain world.

The Democracy Challenge

Throughout the 1990s, the political systems of Central America experienced a profound transformation. For more than 15 years, all of the presidents in Central America have been civilians elected in free and fair elections—having acceded to power from equally legitimate predecessors. Even when the debate over the depth and quality of democracy in the region continues, consensus exists over the improved levels of pluralism and political stability that the countries in the region are enjoying for the first time in their history.

Ironically, the expansion of democracy and democratic values at the end of the Cold War constitutes a big challenge in the relations between the U.S. and Central America. The advent of peace has meant the arrival of new needs and demands arising from social groups that are increasingly organized. In the aftermath of the peace plan it was possible to implement broad and relatively cheap social relief programs to respond to the short-term requirements of hundreds and even thousands of people displaced by violence. With the advent of political normalization and the gradual acceptance of the rule of law, the measures necessary to curb poverty and social exclusion, promote human sustainable development, or ensure democratic governance require long-term approaches that are costly and complex, particularly at a time when strategic priorities, redefined after 9-11, lay elsewhere.

Furthermore, as democracy widens, and more and more social sectors are drawn into its decision-making processes, it also becomes more difficult to control and even to manipulate. This is furthered by the proliferation of news media, stimulated by enhanced freedom of the press legislation. Hence, the more pluralistic Central American societies become, the less likely they are to abide by the rules of traditional politicking. Increasing accountability demands from the public and the vociferous mood of the media have also meant less opportunity for government officials to hide their wrongdoings. More participation, expanded transparency, and no impunity to offenders are new—although not necessarily the predominant—rules of the game.

This gradual, albeit progressive, abandonment of social tolerance for those who hold power or are in office (whose historical origin is probably found in long-standing trends of repression and fear) has been heightened by a generalized decline in satisfaction with democracy throughout Latin America. While faith in democracy has been generally maintained in Central America, contrary to hemispheric standards, the same polls indicate alarmingly low levels of interpersonal confidence throughout the region, particularly on matters relating to corruption (see Table 3.3).[13]

Undoubtedly, corruption in public office—with or without linkages to the private sector, either national or transnational—has become a fundamental factor in U.S.–Central American relations. Moral and ethical considerations aside, corrupt government practices are a threat to democratic governance and political stability because they undermine citizen credibility and, if pervasive, inhibit the normal and efficient administration of

Table 3.3 Interpersonal Confidence in Central America.
Question: In general, would you say that it is possible to trust the majority of people or that one can never be careful enough in interacting with others. Percentages responding that "One can trust the majority of people. (Percentages)

	1996	1997	1998	2000	2001	2002	2003	2004	2005
Costa Rica	11	30	34	13	12	14	11	8	−3
El Salvador	23	30	21	16	14	21	12	16	−7
Guatemala	28	29	26	17	11	14	18	14	−14
Honduras	25	28	16	9	12	15	18	20	−6
Nicaragua	20	35	11	11	31	17	18	12	−8
Panama	25	20	18	15	24	28	25	20	−6

Source: www.latinobarometro.org

public affairs. Consider the views of one U.S. official who clearly voiced his frustration with public probity in Nicaragua. Assistant Secretary of State for Western Hemisphere Affairs Roger F. Noriega asserted that the situation there resembled "… the tug of war between two political dinosaurs who regard politics as a license to steal."[14] Mr. Noriega's claim could very well be valid for many other countries in Central America.[15]

Corruption is also expensive and, overall, a burden that impinges upon the adequate functioning of the free market. It welcomes bad investors, fosters disloyal competition, increases the costs of production, and inhibits the development of good, decent, and world-class best practices. It also invites government intrusions in a realm that some believe should be kept from undue state intervention.

Democratic governance in Central America is also threatened by a dramatic rise in common and organized crime. The region shares this characteristic with Latin America. During the 1990s Latin America became the world's most violent region, with homicide rates of 23 per 10,000 inhabitants, twice as much as world standards and equal to those in war-torn Africa.

Paradoxically, for Central America crime became a growing concern once the civil wars of the 1980s were over and democratic normalization began to take hold. This phenomenon was clearly associated with the imperfect demobilization processes of thousands of combatants (soldiers and irregular fighters alike) who could not be reinstalled in productive activities in countries affected by the war. The availability of men whose only trade had been war for over a decade, combined with a surplus of mostly automatic weapons that quickly fed a surging and eager black market, explains the appearance of dozens of violent gangs in Guatemala, El Salvador, Honduras, and Nicaragua, mostly devoted to kidnappings, bank robberies, extortion, weapons smuggling, and car theft.[16] By 2004, Guatemala was spending more than $200 million dollars a year in private security services, equivalent to 10% of its central government's budget, much more than the country's total investment in public security.[17]

Hence, uncurtailed common and organized crime have significant impacts upon the political quality of Central American democracies. They delegitimize state institutions; they favor the appearance of authoritarian solutions (the so-called *mano dura* or super *mano dura* policies implemented in El Salvador and Honduras), and they have degenerative effects on civil society, mainly by eroding the quality of life in urban communities where people become hostage to fear.

High crime rates also affect the economy and therefore hamper the possibility of Central America's future sustainability. First, violence and insecurity scare away tourists, one of the region's most important sources of revenue, second only to remittances. Second, it reduces the likelihood of investments because it increases the risk factor. Third, it diminishes the productivity of the work force. In sum, crime constitutes an inhibitor of development and economic growth and therefore threatens the overall evolution toward what in the 1990s seemed to be a promising future for Central America.

The United States has been increasingly concerned with public security in Central America as a political issue that affects democratic development and could eventually threaten the United States' own national security objectives. In so doing, it has clearly positioned public security and democratic governance in Central America as matters whose simultaneous domestic and international (intermestic) implications merit particular federal government attention.

Drug trafficking was tackled first. In the 1980s, the United States began a sophisticated and relentless campaign against illegal narcotics trafficking. This campaign expanded and became a truly strategic priority once the linkages between drugs and other kinds of organized crime and insurgency activities in Colombia and its neighbors became apparent. The terrorist activities of the Colombian cartels in the mid-1990s, as well as the increasingly obvious influx of drug money into the political arena (by way of campaign financing and outright personal contributions to notorious political figures) only heightened American fears. This resulted in one of the United States' most decisive foreign policy decisions toward Latin America: the enactment of Plan Colombia.

Central America played an early and significant role in U.S. drug interdiction programs because of its geographic location. A good part of the Colombian drug traffic to the United States passes through the Central American isthmus, and therefore the implementation of effective policies on the matter was crucial to its reduction. According to well-informed sources, U.S.–Central American drug interdiction efforts, while unable to stop drug trafficking altogether, are considered to be increasingly successful and will continue to expand in the foreseeable future (Table 3.4).[18]

Yet the tentacles of illegal drug trafficking have infiltrated a whole array of other criminal activities, all of which undermine democratic institutions. Money laundering, weapons smuggling, prostitution, and human trafficking are frequently related to illegal drug operations. The exchange of guns for drugs between Central America and Colombia is well documented, and preventing the use of "dirty" money to feed extra-continental terrorist organizations is now one of the FBI's explicit priorities.[19]

The case of urban juvenile gangs is similar, particularly those associated with Central American immigrants in the United States, such as the Mara Salvatrucha (MS) and the Mara 18. Formerly found in Los Angeles, these organizations have expanded throughout almost all the territorial United

Table 3.4 Total Drug Seizures: Cocaine, Marijuana, Heroin (kilograms)

	1998	1999	2000	2001
Costa Rica	7,749	3,357	3,180	4,318
Panama	28,323	4,181	9,199	2,294
El Salvador	315	954	879	N/A
Belize	1,597	429	263	4,095
Nicaragua	5,362	2,136	1,696	2,719
Guatemala	9,624	10,752	1,749	4,636
Honduras	3,343	2,314	2,277	N/A

Source: http://www.usdoj.gov/dea/pubs/intel.htm

States. Owing to heightened deportation practices on the part of the U.S. Department of Homeland Security, they have also settled in, and are now a significant part of, the criminal landscapes of Mexico and three Central American countries: Guatemala, El Salvador, and Honduras.[20]

The operation in the United States of gangs largely formed by immigrants is not a new phenomenon. It can be traced all the way back to the mid-nineteenth century when it became one of the salient byproducts of the European flows of people who inundated America. The operation of the Mafia and mafia-like organizations in the first half of the twentieth century, as well as the significant evolution of their financial networks after World War II, are documented facts that have dominated the concerns and travails of U.S. law enforcement agencies for decades.

Nevertheless, the global implications of organized crime, including *maras*, in the age of the Internet has turned gangs into likely agents of non-state violence. For the record, the Bureau for Immigration and Customs Enforcement (ICE) has voiced skepticism regarding some public speculation alleging links between the MS and global terrorist organizations such as Al Qaeda. Yet many government officials in Central America and even high-level members of the U.S. Department of Defense continue to regard gangs as potentially proto-terrorist entities (much like the Colombian drug cartels during the 1980s) that ought to be eliminated for the sake of democratic consolidation.[21] Such views constitute one of the most pervasive policy drivers in the contemporary U.S.–Central America agenda.

The policy options for the United States with regard to the domestic political order in Central America therefore seem to be limited, and eventually complicated, owing to one unavoidable fact: they will all require the United States to tolerate and even stimulate greater, not lesser, degrees of political openness. At times this could mean the acceptance of enhanced civil liberties, which could lead to unrestrained disorder or social turbu-lence. If the United States is once again swept into isolationism or if some new major issue (such as fighting terrorism, as was the case with com-munism before) seizes the U.S. foreign policy agenda to the point of mini-mizing other longer-term structural concerns—such as democracy—then Central America's political opening could be short-lived.

Dealing with the small Central American post–Cold War democratic governments poses a significant, yet paradoxical, challenge for a regional hegemon such as the United States. In order to be consistent with its own rhetoric, the United States should feel compelled to abide by the rule of law, support the local authorities, and uphold their domestic decisions. They also have to take into consideration and respect domestic legal jurispru-dence. Furthermore, imperfect as they may be, in the postmodern world, U.S. democratic allies often exercise their right to disagree, and even engage in active and at times annoying, international protests against their most powerful neighbor.

Central America has already given proof of this in specific cases deal-ing with trade issues or even within the very sensitive realm of the United Nations' General Assembly and Security Council. Several countries in the region have repeatedly voted against the United States' unilateral actions worldwide, or against U.S.-sponsored resolutions regarding sanctions to so-called rogue states. In the region, only Costa Rica and El Salvador have refrained from reestablishing diplomatic relations with Cuba, but even they have rejected U.S. arguments in favor of the continuation of the economic embargo against the Castro regime. Similarly, it has not been easy for the Central American presidents to get the legislative authorization required to undertake joint antidrug operations with U.S. forces. Throughout the 1990s, American diplomats had to struggle to obtain Central American support for U.S. resolutions in matters pertaining to issues related to the environment, labor, and birth control.

Yet, while sensitive to those demands, in the post 9-11 context, the U.S. government will continue to exercise its hegemonic powers to privilege its own security and political interests above any others. Hence, it has been quick to disengage itself from, and has even outspokenly criticized, some Central American governments' positions on sensitive questions includ-ing national elections, internal security, judicial performance, the man-agement of land conflicts affecting U.S. citizens, and the like.

The old U.S. "big stick" seems to be working as effectively in the age of the Internet as it did in the years of gunboat diplomacy.

In the final analysis, the United States will continue to struggle with democracy in Central America because it is messy, legislatures have minds of their own, and presidents, ministers, and their advisors are not always reliable partners whose legitimacy can be taken for granted. During much of the 1980s, Central America learned this lesson in dealing with the many actors who participate in the making of U.S. foreign policy toward the region. Now it is the United States' turn to work through the complexity of shared governance in Central America.

Can the changes that are taking place in the political systems and within the marketplace be assimilated fast enough by countries with weak political institutions? Can the highly centralized but equally weak and inefficient Central American states respond to the demands of an awakened and more demanding civil society? Can this be done in a context of structural reform and declining social investments? These are some of the most daunting questions of our time.

Social and Economic Issues

Central America is one of the poorest regions in the hemisphere. Three of every five Central Americans live in conditions of poverty, and two of every five are indigent or in extreme poverty.[22] Against this backdrop, it is not surprising that democracy has been slow in taking hold and that democratic governance remains feeble.[23]

Several factors explain this endemic condition that derives in part from the very nature of the Central American economies, historically driven by low-cost, transnationally controlled exports of primary products such as coffee, sugar cane, and bananas. The political and social structures emerging from this economic order produced gross inequalities within the Central American population early on. They also profited from a vicious cycle of deprivation that, with the notable exception of Costa Rica, prevented the development of a significant upwardly mobile bourgeoisie and ultimately the consolidation of a more democratic and pluralistic political culture.

Widely acknowledged as a burden on the future of the region and its political elites, the traditional "dessert" exports began to be diversified during the 1960s and 1970s. At the time, the Central American Common Market was in place, and the isthmus seemed destined to greater levels of prosperity under the aegis of import substitution and incipient industrialization. Successful for over a decade, the ascent of regional integration came to an abrupt end after a 3-day war (and the ensuing 25 years' rift) between Honduras and El Salvador in 1969. Yet for the Central American poor, the integration stalemate had little, if any, significance other than that it left hundreds of thousands of displaced, uneducated, and ill-nourished rural inhabitants, barely surviving in the outskirts of the unprepared urban centers to which they flocked seeking the mirage of a better life. Social conditions did not improve during the years of turmoil and violence that followed, and by the end of the conflict in the late 1980s, living conditions in Central America on the average had deteriorated to 1940 standards.

Economic diversification finally took hold in the wake of political normalization. Stimulated by new global economic trends, Central America became aware of the changing international environment and began a frantic search for innovative products and new markets. Hence the boom of nontraditional exports ("other desserts"—melons, watermelons, mangos—vegetables and tubers, flowers, seafood, textiles, and electronics and high-tech components), the provision of services (through call centers mainly in Costa Rica and baking mainly in Panama), and a strong and largely successful effort to enhance tourism, an industry that became the region's second most important revenue source by the turn of the century (Tables 3.5 and 3.6).

However, the renewed prosperity did not bring about a major transformation of social conditions. Moreover, while poverty standards improved with respect to the 1980s and 1990s in the early twenty-first century, the inequality gap widened, as the Central American countries were unable or unwilling to address the key components of any serious effort toward the creation of societies of opportunity: better income distribution, enhanced levels of public education, the provision of adequate health services, and the implementation of policies aimed at some of the region's longstanding deficits: low-income housing, urban sanitation, environmental degradation, and public security.

Among the many problems that this latest phase of the Central American economic modernization produced was the massification of low-wage

Table 3.5 Importance of Tourism in Central America (2000 estimates)

Country	% Total Exports	%Total Jobs	Capital Investments (Millions of $)	% Total Investment
Costa Rica	4.2	17.2	608.9	17.1
El Salvador	2.3	8.9	237.0	9.6
Guatemala	3.3	17.0	375.7	10.4
Honduras	3.0	9.4	179.6	12.2
Nicaragua	2.9	13.5	58.4	6.9
Panama	5.1	12.3	379.3	12.4

Source: World Travel and Tourism Council, in PNUD (Programa de las Naciones Unidas para del Desarrollo), Segundo Informe sobre Desarrollo Humano en Centroamérica y Panamá, San José, 2003, p. 143.

Table 3.6 International Tourist Arrivals (in thousands) and Tourism Receipts (US$ millions)

	2000		2001		2002		2003 estimate	
	Arrivals	Receipts	Arrivals	Receipts	Arrivals	Receipts	Arrivals	Receipts
Belize	196	122	196	120	200	130	221	156
Costa Rica	1088	1302	1131	1173	1113	1161	1239	1293
El Salvador	795	217	735	201	951	245	857	226
Guatemala	826	482	835	562	884	620	880	621
Honduras	471	260	518	256	550	301	611	337
Nicaragua	486	129	483	135	472	135	526	151
Panama	484	458	519	486	534	528	566	585

Source: World Tourism Organization: http://www.world-tourism.org/facts/menu.html.

employment, a factor strongly associated with the rising inequality patterns in the region.[24] Indeed, the boom of mostly foreign-owned textile *maquila* (assembly) industries in Guatemala, El Salvador, Honduras, and Nicaragua undoubtedly provided employment opportunities for hundreds of thousands of workers (mainly women) and alleviated their families' poverty. Yet these industries draw on Central America's low labor standards and wages to be competitive, thus consolidating the pattern of limited social development that continued to inhibit the region's much needed human progress. This pattern became further strained by the emergence of China as one of the fiercest—and most competitive—actors in the low-wage markets worldwide after 2005. As it stands, in all likelihood, China will severely hamper (and eventually stop altogether) the continuing success of Central America's textile *maquilas* in only a few years (Table 3.7).

The large proportion of informal workers in Central America, along with their access to training and education, also remains a major midterm challenge that should be addressed as part of the region's efforts to improve the quality of life of its inhabitants.[25]

Against this backdrop, the United States' social and economic cooperation programs since the 1960s are not negligible. The United States has neither been indifferent to, nor ignorant of, the region's needs. For decades, the U.S. government has contributed significantly through USAID and other official agencies in support of the Central American efforts to improve social standards and alleviate the region's most pressing humanitarian demands (Table 3.8). Up until the 1990s, the United States was Central America's most important international donor, a status only briefly lost to the European Union, whose enhanced interest in the region after 1984 waned once the crisis abated and its own post–Cold War agenda took hold.,,,,

Table 3.7 Central America: Exports with Maquila and without Maquila (2002) (millions of current U.S. $ and percentage)

	With Maquila	%	Without Maquila	%
Central America	2,831	16.4%	2831	27.8%
United States	11,087	64.1%	3965	38.9%
European Union	1,550	9.0%	1550	15.2%
Others	1,839	10.6%	1839	18.1%
Total	17,307	100%	101,85	100%

Source: SIECA (Secretariat for Central American Economic Integration) and U.S. Trade Representative in PNUD, *Segundo Informe sobre Desarrollo Humano en Centroamérica y Panamá*, San José, 2003, p. 173.

Table 3.8 Total USAID Funds (in thousands of dollars)

	FY 2004	FY 2005	FY 2006
Nicaragua	41,707	47,068	41,390
Guatemala	43,456	46,481	39,863
Panama	6,622	8,101	8,604
El Salvador	34,935	34,565	25,354
Honduras	43,024	48,913	44,965

Source: http://www.usaid.gov/policy/budget/cbj2006/lac/.

U.S. cooperation has experienced important transformations. The old reformist approach that once dominated the Alliance for Progress, and the Cold War emphasis on social programs being necessary yet subordinate elements of counter-insurgency campaigns, became void once the Cold War ended. While still dominant during the early Reagan years, these traditional approaches were soon profoundly upset by the impact of neo-conservative doctrines. Indeed, the rediscovery of the free market as the driving force for social progress brought about a new generation of proposals that definitively ended over four decades of international welfare programs. The 1984 Caribbean Basin Initiative was the first, most notorious, and significant example of this evolving trend.

The bipartisan support for "trade not aid," heralded, though still timidly, by the Kissinger Commission's Report in the mid-1980s was one of the 1990s most pervasive changes in U.S. foreign policy. Facing growing deficits during the Reagan–Bush period, and unwilling to upset the budgetary balances achieved under Clinton, Republicans and Democrats alike saw in enhanced free trade and the strengthening of the internal markets the perfect recipe for economic prosperity and democratic consolidation abroad. Thus, they called for the lifting of trade restrictions and the reduction of regulatory systems hampering U.S. investments. In addition, they insisted on ensuring functional legal systems that would not subject U.S. business to uncertain, unfair rules of the game, and they earnestly believed that "trickle-down" economics would be capable of promoting the social progress and political stability still lacking after decades of state-sponsored, corrupt, and largely unsuccessful paternalism.

The U.S. recipe for social development in Central America is challenged by the region's concrete conditions. In one critical area, that of public education, the situation is so dismal that it could not possibly be addressed by minor public policy measures complemented by the private sector, regardless of how massive these complementary resources may be. One of every three Central Americans 15 years or older is illiterate. The situation is worse in Guatemala and Nicaragua, among women, in rural areas, and within the indigenous population. Recent statistics show that one in every five children from 7 to 12 years of age and three in every five teenagers are not registered in school. From each thousand students entering the first grade, only 604 successfully finish their primary cycle of six years. However, they take 8.5 calendar years to complete it, or 1.4 years per grade. One in every four schools has only one teacher, but one-teacher schools take care of as much as 5% of the total student population. Almost 25% of Central American preschool, primary school, and secondary school teachers do not hold a degree. In a dramatic turn of events, even in Costa Rica 40% of all teenagers are not attending high school.[26]

This is only to be expected, given that the expenditure in all educational levels, on average, is around 3.4% of the national GDP, most of which is directed toward paying low salaries, leaving very little else to be invested in materials and other didactic resources. Specialists have repeatedly voiced their concern about this insufficient allocation of funds for education. They have warned that unless education expenditures are doubled, the region will further lose its competitiveness in an ever-expanding world economy in search of a well-educated, highly competitive work force.[27]

The burden of two hundred years of deprivation and social exclusion will continue to hamper Central America in its foreseeable future. While great expectations have been placed upon free trade, the truth of the matter is that unless the Central American governments and political elites are able (and willing) to address the region's most serious social deficits through the implementation of comprehensive national development strategies, there will be little benefit from the enhanced wealth that global markets are supposed to generate.

Indeed, some troubling questions remain unanswered: will the momentum of trade liberalization be enough to break the historical inertia of the Central American economies and their highly exploitative nature? Will the demands of an increasingly competitive international context, driven by technology and rapidly multiplying knowledge, allow Central America to abandon its current low-wage, environment-blind, socially irresponsible productive systems and adopt a more rational, service-oriented perspective within the context of more socially accountable democracies?

Interestingly enough, the United States and Central America have explored common strategies to address these and other questions in the past. The Kissinger Commission was the first of many efforts jointly undertaken with that purpose. Soon after the report was made public in 1984, another commission was created by the U.S. Congress under the leadership of Senator Terry Sanford (D-NC). Known by its founder's name and composed of distinguished U.S. and Central American citizens, the Sanford

Commission helped raise the awareness of the region in the United States at a time when attention on the isthmus was beginning to fade away. While different from the Kissinger Commission in that it proposed a multinational approach to development cooperation for Central America (it called for the substantive participation of Western Europe, the Nordic countries, and Japan in the reconstruction efforts), the Sanford Commission's recommendations were only partially implemented, thus truncating its stated goals (Table 3.9).

Recent studies of regional development emphasize the existence of a three-tiered Central America. The first, most developed, region is formed by Panama and Costa Rica, the second is formed by El Salvador and

Table 3.9 Main Recommendations of the Sanford Commission

Immediate Action

Focus on refugees and displaced persons in extreme poverty.

Make special provisions for children under five, pregnant and nursing women, and the elderly.

Generate productive employment by focusing on food security, health, nutrition, basic education, safe drinking water and sanitation, temporary housing, infrastructure, and human rights.

Sustained Development

Conserve the region's fragile natural resources.

Encourage growth, increased employment, and improved distribution of wealth.

Aggressively expand and diversify exports.

Refurbish and strengthen the Central American Common Market.

Reinstate a common tariff structure that gradually and deliberately reduces protection of domestic industry. The strategic importance of national food security and rural employment, however, justifies some protection for rice, corn, and beans.

Reform the tax systems and financial policies and revise agrarian policies.

Reform the region's schools, placing highest priority on spending for primary education.

Restore and reform Central America's health systems, particularly in rural areas.

Source: The Report of the International Commission for Central American Recovery and Development, *Poverty, Conflict and Hope: A Turning Point in Central America*, Durham, NC: Duke University Press, 1989.

Guatemala, and the last by Nicaragua and Honduras. These tiers, seg-mented along human development strata, are proof of the wide asym-metries that continue to plague the region and of the complexity of the pending tasks ahead. Moreover, given that enormous differences are also pervasive within each of the Central American countries, tackling the social agenda would require a sophisticated and well-financed approach. Is this likely without massive tax reforms, sound income redistribution policies, and a degree of international solidarity that seems not to be avail-able for the moment?

The United States continues to be engaged in this dilemma. In March 2002 President George W. Bush called for a "new compact for growth and development" that he proposed should be implemented within the boundaries of the Millennium Challenge Account (MCA), a new initiative through which development assistance would be provided to countries that rule justly, invest in their people, and encourage economic freedom. So far, three Central American countries (El Salvador, Honduras, and Nicaragua) have been granted significant MCA funds amounting to more than $500 million dollars for fiscal years 2005–2008.[28]

Whether this is achieved in time to not lose the momentum produced by democratization and the advent of peace is yet to be seen. During the past few years, many formally democratic governments in Latin America were overthrown by infuriated citizens fed up by corruption and wide-spread social deprivation. Limited private sector social responsibility and dependency on foreign capital could stimulate this phenomenon in Central America, given the exasperation produced by unanswered social demands and the increasing popular discontent with government perfor-mance. Thus, in many ways, it will be political will and the quality of the Central American leadership (not to say the strength and credibility of state institutions), not globalization, entrepreneurship, or the openness of the market, that will ultimately determine the nature, scope, and demo-cratic condition of the fundamental transformations that Central America so urgently requires.

Migration

More than a million Central Americans were displaced by war during the 1980s, one of the many negative unintended consequences of the regional conflict.[29] Most of these migrants, mainly Guatemalan, Honduran, Sal-vadoran, and Nicaraguan nationals left their countries for Mexico, the United States, Belize, or Costa Rica. Once the military conflicts ended, the migrant flow continued largely because of economic, not political, reasons.[30] Over two million Central Americans live in the United States, nearly 50% of whom are from El Salvador. Salvadorans have also found land and created opportunities in Belize, which is now home to 30,000 Salvadorans in a total population of less than 250,000 people. Nicaraguans represent at least 10% of the total population of Costa Rica. These "fresh diasporas" constitute important elements in both the domestic and foreign policies of the United States and the countries of the region.[31]

Central American integration into the global economy is being fostered in part through the efforts of these diasporic groups. Critical dimensions of the integration include tourism, telecommunications, and nostalgic trade. Tourism throughout Central America has been enhanced by the return of nationals who visit their countries. It is reported that Central American tourists returning to their countries have an average length of stay of over two weeks and spend at least $50 a day.

Advanced telecommunications and new technologies have facilitated a whole new sector in the U.S. economy for calling cards—prepaid long-distance phone cards that sell access to the region on a commodity, bulk discount logic. Increased contact has also led to a new market in the United States for the services and goods that can be found in the home-land. Thus, nationally produced items such as beer, cheese, vegetables, *pupusas, empanadas*, and rum have found spots on the shelves of U.S. grocery stores, as more and more of their shoppers attempt to maintain their homeland connections and as the market for ethnic foods in the United States expands.[32] Furthermore, it is now common to find Central American specialty restaurants in Washington, Miami, and Chicago. A major Guatemala chicken venue has opened its first store in Los Angeles on its way to China and Indonesia, where it is expected to open 50 and 100 restaurants, respectively. This company, founded in 1971, now sports more than 200 franchises in Mexico, the United States, and Central America.[33]

Central American immigration to the United States has two major policy dimensions. The first issue is legal. Immigration constitutes a significant challenge to the U.S. justice system because of the confusing status of so many from the region.[34] The Central American governments as well as migrant and humanitarian organizations have tried to impede the massive deportation of undocumented Central Americans back to their countries of origin. Lacking the resources and political clout of their Mexican counterparts, these efforts have largely been unsuccessful.

Massive deportations of Central American criminals from the United States to their countries of origin have had a serious—yet undesired—outcome in Central America. Many of these individuals are members of gangs in the United States, such as Mara Salvatrucha (MS) and Mara 18, and upon return to their countries, they tend to recreate their criminal networks. Governments and the media in the isthmus tend to concur that the

Maras are to blame for most of the 10,000 murders that occur in Central America every year. In 2002 this amounted to 28 killings per 10,000 inhabitants, five times the murder rate in the United States in the same period. Police estimates indicate that Mara membership amounts to 14,000 people in Guatemala, 10,500 in El Salvador, 36,000 in Honduras, 2,600 in Costa Rica, and 1,400 in Panama. This phenomenon has also been replicated in Southern Mexico, particularly along the border with Guatemala, where the numbers have increased dramatically since 2004.[35]

According to the *Christian Science Monitor*, Maras now account for more than half of all violent crimes committed in Honduras and El Salvador and have become the third leading source of violence in Guatemala. Some contention exists as to the legitimacy of these claims that some consider repeat "government propaganda" to justify a strong-fisted (and very popular) public security strategy that ignores the social dimension of criminality. However, the truth of the matter is that the problem is by no means negligible. Currently, Mara-related activity stands at the top of the public security agenda in Central America and has become a major source of concern to U.S. law enforcement agencies.

Questions revolve around the status of an estimated 400,000 undocumented Central Americans in the country and another 370,000 who are classified under the Temporary Protected Status (TPS)[36] that has been periodically renewed under both Presidents Clinton and Bush.[37] However, there is almost universal support in the region for a continuation of the TPS classification to renew the temporary immigration status of migrants from El Salvador, Honduras, and Nicaragua, whose presence in the country can be linked to the natural disasters of the late 1990s and early 2000, such as Hurricane Mitch and a devastating earthquake in El Salvador.[38]

The second dimension of migration is financial and has a direct and extraordinary impact upon the national economies of the Central American countries. Central American immigrants send billions of dollars annually to their countries of origin in the form of remittances. California, New York, Texas, Florida, and Illinois tend to be major source states for remittances to all of Latin America and the Caribbean. California accounts for some $9 billion in remittances, but states such as Iowa ($69 million) and Kentucky ($53 million) send millions as well. Remittances from Salvadorans working in the United States sent to family members are a major source of foreign income for the country, accounting for nearly $2.5 billion in 2004. Guatemala is close behind, collecting nearly $1.5 billion, and Honduras and Nicaragua receive nearly $1 billion each.

In the case of El Salvador and Nicaragua, these remittances represent more than 10% of GDP, much more than what the countries get from the international community by way of donations for development. In El Salvador foreign remittances are higher than the revenues produced by coffee exports[39] and are not only used by families on an individual basis, but have also become significant sources of community development.[40]

The combined social and financial impact that a massive return of Central Americans currently living in the United States would have upon their countries of origin is unimaginable. No country in the region would have the capacity to offer their nationals and their children the services and employment opportunities they would require to resettle. As mentioned above, the deportation of Central Americans linked to street gangs in major U.S. cities has already proved to place great strain on the fabric of Central American life.

The Central American community in the United States is highly fragmented and has a very limited capacity to mobilize political and financial support to rally its cause. This is evident in that the Central American "lobby" is mostly performed by European and even North American nongovernmental organizations.[41] This situation leaves the immigration question basically in the hands of domestic agencies and policy-makers, who have little regard for the interests of the affected countries. As a consequence, the debate over immigration is largely driven by domestic concerns in the United States, such as the impact of immigrants on public health, their role in the labor force, their impact on domestic employment and wage levels, and the additional cost in education and social welfare they produce on the U.S. infrastructure.

The immigration challenge is a significant ongoing source of tension between the United States and the region. It will continue to be so in the first decades of the twenty-first century largely because there is little likelihood that the flow of immigrants—with and without documents—will abate given the poverty and shortage of opportunities at all levels of the wage spectrum.

The Economy and Trade

If the countries of Central America decided to merge today, their combined economic impact on the United States would be, at best, very limited. Their market absorbs less than 2% of all exports from the United States. Their total annual output would be less than that of Miami-Dade County Florida, and their leading export to the United States would not be goods or services, but people, who would be their biggest source of foreign exchange—about $6 billion annually. The region's economy is based on traditional and nontraditional agricultural exports (coffee, bananas, sugar, winter vegetables, and flowers), textile assembly, and tourism. While it has had some success in the diversification of its economy beyond primary agricultural products during the past three decades, pervasive poverty and underemployment give job creation an urgency for any government in power.

As noted earlier, economic integration has been one of the continuing discussions in the region since at least the early 1800s. There is a general recognition throughout the region that the small size of each economy is a critical impediment to regional or global competitiveness. Markets are limited, and a skilled labor force is in short supply.[42] The Central American Common Market, established in the mid-1960s, had only limited success in the region but was torn apart by the "soccer-war" between Honduras and El Salvador in 1969. Since then, Europe's move toward a unified market, the Reagan-era Caribbean Basin Initiative (giving the region improved access to the U.S. market), the Common Market of the Southern Cone (MERCO-SUR) (bringing together Brazil, Chile, Paraguay, Argentina, and Uruguay in a customs union), the North American Free Trade Agreement (NAFTA) (opening the markets of Canada, the United States, and Mexico to free trade and a unified investment regime), and the proposed Free Trade Area of the Americas (FTAA) (involving all the countries of the hemisphere except Cuba) have served, among others, as guideposts for improved economic cooperation in the region accompanied by greater access to the U.S. marketplace.[43]

During the Clinton administration, Central America did propose several initiatives to take advantage of the movement toward free trade in the Americas. While the Clinton administration talked market-opening and cooperation, the curtain closed on any important trade initiative in the hemisphere following the signing of NAFTA. Clinton was more interested in appeasing domestic antitrade constituencies during this period, and the Republican Congress would not grant him authority to negotiate trade agreements expeditiously.

The Environmental Challenge

Central America encompasses less than 1% of the world territory yet possesses close to 7% of the planet's biodiversity. The isthmus has more bird and insect species than Europe and North America combined. For these and other reasons, it is a region whose environment is subject to a great deal of interest—both regionally and internationally.[44]

The region has significant environmental challenges. First, every country is suffering from the depletion of forest coverage, which leads to increased soil erosion, the deterioration of watersheds, and decreased biodiversity.[45] It is estimated that the region has lost more than 70% of its forest cover because of overgrazing, agriculture, increased mining, and unregulated logging. In Nicaragua, for example, illegal trafficking in lumber is a growing business. Peasants are paid up to $6 to cut down a hardwood tree that will later sell for up to $1,500 once it is smuggled out of the country.[46]

Second, the basic sanitation infrastructure is so limited that sewage and solid waste treatment is in short supply, and chemical and pesticide run-off into the water supply is common. These problems will multiply as the urban populations in each of the countries continue to grow. While the figures vary across the region, Guatemala is a good example of infrastructural limits: only 3% of its wastewater is treated, and only 53% of households have garbage collection.[47]

Finally, Central America's 4800-mile coastline is rich in mangroves, coral reefs, and other forms of coastal and marine ecosystems. Their fragility is even more complicated as a result of agricultural and industrial runoff and untreated sewage.

It should come as no surprise that Central America's ecosystems are under stress. Most countries of the region have only recently developed environmental laws, and they have even less ability to enforce what is on the books. Governmental environmental agencies have limited funding, few trained staff, and negligible enforcement capability. In the countryside, justice officials may not even know the laws, much less be able to enforce them.

The environmental challenges facing the region explain the high profile these issues had in the drafting of the Central American–United States of America Joint Declaration (CONCA—USA) in 1994 and why they became the centerpiece of that initiative once it was enacted. Additional interest resulted from the attention of countless governmental and nongovernmental organizations, which have significant political influence in Congress. Once again, the intermestic nature of environmental policies moved them to the forefront of foreign policy decision-making.

The U.S. Agency for International Development has had numerous long-standing environmental initiatives in the region. The most consequential is the Regional Environmental Program for Central America (PROARCA), which was created on the heels of the CONCA–USA initiative in the mid-1990s. Since 1996, PROARCA has focused on conservation and natural resource management in the region. Now, during its next five-year period, it is focusing on the Mesoamerican Biological Corridor (CBM) and four general issues: initiatives that improve the management of protected areas, expanded access to markets for environmentally friendly products and services, harmonization of environmental laws, and increasing the use of less polluting technologies and practices.[48]

Under any scenario of change during the next few years in U.S.–Central American affairs, it is clear that environmental issues will continue to be major components of the regional dialogue. In many respects, they are the quintessential intermestic issues. The more closely linked they can be to U.S. security, the greater the likelihood that they will be of more than a passing interest to U.S. decision-makers.

The United States, Central America, and the Rest of the Hemisphere

U.S.–Central American relations should be analyzed in the broader context of their hemispheric associations. These associations have experienced profound changes over the past few years and remain complex owing to an ever-growing agenda of unprecedented challenges.

The creation of MERCOSUR and its gradual extension to include other associated countries have altered the geopolitical continental balance. Brazil and the United States (and their respective zones of influence) have become entangled in a not-so-quiet battle to determine the final format of the FTAA.

Furthermore, South America has recently experienced the comeback of democratically elected, progressive, and even leftist governments in Argentina, Brazil, Chile, Panama, Paraguay, and Uruguay, whose victories sometimes have taken place amidst ferocious global-phobic, anti-U.S. rhetoric. Once in power, these governments have generally taken a moderate course of action, but it is clear that Washington cannot count on their unconditional support in many of its most important international propositions.

Two other cases have become a source of grave concern to U.S. foreign policy-makers. The first is that of Venezuela, one of the most important members of the Association of Caribbean States and a nation riddled by long-standing political instability. Rich in petroleum reserves and ruled by a stridently anti-U.S., pro-Cuba, and extremely popular president who had no qualms about visiting Iraq in the days preceding the U.S. invasion or befriending the Iranian *ayatollahs*, Venezuela has become a matter of particular attention to the Bush Administration, so much so that its most important members—including the president himself—have repeatedly accused Venezuela of being a destabilizing factor in the Americas, and even a likely candidate to join the "Axis of Evil" along with Cuba, Iran, and North Korea. For years now, the U.S. and Venezuelan governments have been entangled in a vociferous campaign of mutual accusations that has led to repeated diplomatic clashes. In several instances, these clashes have involved Colombia, Venezuela's troubled (and troublesome) neighbor and staunch U.S. supporter.

The U.S. government is also following the evolution of Bolivia, Ecuador, and even Peru, whose permanent state of political turmoil and disarray continues to threaten the Andean region's precarious multiethnic republics. Andean instability would have generally not caused any major concerns to Washington, had it not been for the leadership behind the massive popular uprisings that have been able to topple three presidents and put two others in question. These movements are inspired by a profoundly nationalistic rhetoric based in the reclaiming of the indigenous ancestral rights, lands and natural resources, and are mostly led by members of the coca-producing associations in the Bolivian lowlands. These leaders have been able to inflame and organize the majority of the indigenous population against the political elites and their international associates and are now threatening to reverse decades of antidrug policies implemented under the guidance of the United States.

In such a context, the position that Mexico, Central America, the Caribbean Community (CARICOM), and Colombia adopt will have a definitive impact on the construction of a new hemispheric equilibrium. This would be particularly important given the widespread perception that the United States, incapable of forging a continental consensus around the FTAA and other foreign initiatives, will try to impose its preponderance through a "building-bloc" strategy in which northern Latin America would serve as the initial stepping-stone.

Central America undoubtedly looks north—not south—when it assesses its strategic possibilities moving into the twenty-first century. Geopolitical as well as historical affinities explain Central America's commitment to the Northern Hemisphere as its main focus of economic and political attention. Central America also enjoys a preferential relationship with Mexico, a country to which it has been bound since before the arrival of the European *conquistadores*. Mexico's own associations with the United States could therefore provide an interesting backdrop if indeed the region decides to explore—and the United States concurs—additional avenues of bilateral cooperation in the context of a stronger, more integrated North American community. Could Mexico and Central America team up to undertake this extraordinary endeavor? It depends.

Mexico and the United States enjoy a very complex and often paradoxical relationship. Both countries are aware of their mutual dependency, but often they neglect their binational responsibilities. This love–hate, engagement–aloofness pattern does not seem to be diminishing. The expectations created by the almost simultaneous election of George W. Bush and Vicente Fox, two former governors whose personal demeanors and ideological affinities seemed capable of taking the relationship to new heights, have proven a fiasco, largely because of their inability to deal with one—admittedly crucial—issue: immigration.

One renowned analyst of U.S.–Mexico relations has observed that those relations have developed in "automatic pilot" for most of the past six years.

The automatic pilot, he says, "has averted the grave dangers that threaten the US-Mexican relationship. Nevertheless, it has not made them disappear. The relationship has floated, but has not progressed."[49]

Unlikely as it may seem, this disengagement of the United States and its most important Latin American partner constitutes irrefutable proof of the lack of significance the rest of the hemisphere attributes to Washington at a time of heightened security concerns. It also shows the difficulties these other peripheral areas, including Central America, will have in getting Washington's attention, much less action, in the next few years.

However, while the Southern Cone has received sporadic attention, with the exception of Chile, South America remains *terra incognita* for most Central Americans. Therefore, even when for Central America, Mexico, and the Greater Caribbean, the proximity of the United States has been a source of geopolitical domination for most of their modern histories, it has also been an opportunity to establish trade, cooperation, and political partnerships that have facilitated investments and stimulated economic growth even before free trade initiatives took hold as the preferred vehicles for prosperity and development.

In the Andean region and the Southern Cone, the predominance of the United States was equally obtrusive yet lacked the military connotations so pervasive in the Caribbean Basin. Chile, Argentina, and Brazil, not the United States, have played the role of regional hegemon in the Andes and the Basin of the River Plate.

Historical and cultural factors notwithstanding, those differences have to do with the sizes of the countries and their economies. In the Caribbean Basin (aside from Panama and its trans-isthmian canal) only Mexico, Colombia, and Venezuela have had the capacity to call the strategic attention of the United States, either owing to their immediate vicinity (in the case of Mexico) or their massive natural resources, particularly petroleum and large domestic markets.

Thus, as the United States crafts a new relationship with Latin America in a changing geopolitical framework, Central America could play a limited, albeit significant, role as one of the hegemon's preferential allies in an extended NAFTA platform once the Central American Free Trade Agreement ratifications are finally achieved.

Conclusion

During the 1990s, as the Cold War passed into history, Central America was largely left to itself to grapple with major issues—security, democracy, the economy, migration, free trade, and the environment. Under any scenario, a decade is plainly too short a period for significant and lasting changes to occur.

Things changed abruptly on September 11, 2001. On the heels of the attack on the World Trade Center, the United States unabashedly returned to blunt unilateralism, and Central America had little recourse but to return to a more submissive relationship with the United States, albeit one that has greater contradictions, given the deepening of pluralism in the region and the institutionalization of democracy. The more open policy environment of Central America's post–Cold War moment passed during the 1990s with some deepened attention paid to the enduring issues that must be addressed if the region is to improve the standard of living for its people. The fact that these issues lend themselves to an intermestic framework at once complicates the range of options and processes necessary for them to be addressed amicably. The coalitions that form to resolved any given question concerning the region have been transnationalized such that any domestic question in the United States or in Central America has immediate implications one-for-the-other. The range of solutions is now much richer than in any Cold War framework, even if the options available have significantly narrowed as a consequence of 9-11.

CHAPTER 4

CAFTA: A Case Study in Intermestic Politics

Introduction

The Central America–Dominican Republic Free Trade Agreement with the United States (CAFTA) was signed on August 2, 2004. Subject to review and ratification in each of the signatory countries, it is designed to eliminate tariffs and trade barriers as well as expand regional opportunities for their respective workers, manufacturers, consumers, farmers, ranchers, and service providers. Upon ratification, it will immediately eliminate tariffs on more than 80% of U.S. exports of consumer and industrial products, phasing out the remaining 20% over the next two decades.[1] The agreement provides reciprocal access for U.S. products and services.

An examination of U.S.–Central America trade relations involving (CAFTA)[2] offers an excellent case study to illustrate the complex nature of U.S.–Central America relations in the post–Cold War era.

Trade Policy-Making in the United States and Central America

The blunt unilateralism of the United States since 9-11 has resulted in a new antiterrorism security regime in the region. Thus, to promote CAFTA's approval by the U.S. Congress, U.S. policy makers were quick to use the security argument to justify the new trade agreement. A senior foreign policy official said, "We must decide whether to promote America's strategic interests or its special interests."[3]

However, as one observer of the U.S. trade policy scene stated shortly after the Cold War ended, "International trade is mostly a matter of domestic politics," and "the future of the trading system depends on the domestic choices" that industrial and developing countries will make over the next few years.[4]

In the United States, the Constitution gives Congress the final word on foreign trade. For much of the period during and after World War II, the Congress granted to the president and the executive branch the authority to set policy. With the opening of the global economy, trade policy has become the connector between "Main Street" in the United States and markets and producers overseas. International commercial negotiations now involve more than simply setting tariff levels. The debate has moved beyond tariffs in agricultural and industrial products to opening markets for trade in services, the negotiation of labor and environmental standards, product safety, and other internal regulations that have an impact on the well-being, safety, and health of consumers.

The growing U.S. reliance on imports, the transfer of technology and know-how off-shore, and the movement of the American economy from industrial to postindustrial have made trade politics, always intense, even more divisive. A post–World War II bipartisan consensus on foreign (and trade) policy has broken down. With the withdrawal of U.S. military combat troops from Vietnam in 1973, the U.S. Congress rejected the notion that "politics stops at the water's edge" and took a series of initiatives to reengage more directly in foreign policy decision-making. Among other reasons, there was an understanding that "it is inextricably related to domestic pocketbook issues...."[5] In the process, the U.S. Congress itself emerged as a world power in co-determining the shape and direction of foreign policy issues with the executive branch and the president.

As a consequence, a cycle of mutual suspicion has emerged that is almost circular in nature:

> Congress doesn't trust the Executive branch to be tough enough on foreigners and to look out for U.S. commercial interests at home or abroad. The Executive branch assumes that many members of Congress will simply protect narrow constituent interests rather than the national interest. Labor, environmental and consumer groups think that business and government trade negotiators ignore their concerns and are anti-democratic. Business suspects the motives of NGO's (non-governmental organizations), assuming they will be obstructionist or absolutist.[6]

Under these circumstances, trade policy-making is immediately politicized, taking on complex transnational and intermestic dimensions.

In Central America trade policy-making had traditionally been isolated in the hands of a few elites in and out of government. Prior to the end of the Cold War, the Ministries of Foreign Affairs and Economics took the lead in conjunction with exporters' associations and the dominant importers. As the Cold War subsided and markets opened to foreign trade, power over foreign trade decision-making was often contested between the traditional diplomatic bureaucracies of the Ministry of Foreign Affairs and the newly created Ministry of Foreign Trade, possibly in conjunction with an association or confederation of industries or exporters. Normally these ministries hired younger, more formally trained economists and lawyers who moved fluidly in and out of the public and private sector, often provoking perceptions of conflicts of interest.

During the 1990s, however, as groups and interests in civil society throughout the region began to enjoy new levels of openness, and as technology and advanced communication became democratized, these same groups could instantaneously connect with like-minded affiliates in other countries, in both the region and elsewhere, with similar interests. As the movement for open markets, free trade, and economic integration picked up during the 1980s and early 1990s (the Uruguay Round in 1986, the Single European Market in 1992, the North American Free Trade Agreement [NAFTA] in 1993), these same groups allied with counterparts in the United States and elsewhere in Europe. Intermestic politics around trade issues was born.

Although not involving U.S.–Central American trade issues per se, a significant milestone in intermestic dynamics occurred in 1999 in Seattle, Washington. There, at the Third Ministerial Meeting of the World Trade Organization (WTO), nongovernmental groups protested business-led market-opening initiatives as an undemocratic, nonaccountable style of decision-making leading to expanded trade. An estimated 1000 activist groups from around the world had signed on to the anti-WTO campaign.[7] Seattle ushered in a new and more intense phase of intermestic trade policy and was a harbinger of intensified debate over expanded trade in the Americas.

While the WTO was the immediate target of demonstrations in 1999, the trade negotiations arena had become the magnet for interests and groups who often had conflicting concerns about the changing nature of global affairs. The emergent coalitions included alliances of environmentalists (who seek to enhance protections against further local and global ecosystem depredation), fair traders (who want to limit competition for jobs from workers in poor countries), human rights groups (who fear that expanded trade results in child labor violations and labor exploitation more generally), consumer rights groups (who worry about floods of unsafe products), sovereignty-obsessed nationalists (who fight to protect encroachment on decision-making from nonnational organizations), and others who may just be chronically dissatisfied with the place of change in a context of continued market opening.[8]

Consequently, antitrade activists have learned that they do have influence. They have used the gatherings of multilateral organizations and the issues presented by free traders as an opportunity to have an impact on trade policy decision-making. The hemispheric-wide movement for a Free Trade Agreement of the Americas (FTAA) in the early and mid-1990s was one arena allowing this hyper-mobilization of interests to occur, but as the FTAA bogged down, another opportunity presented itself—this time focusing on Central America.

CAFTA

The advent of a Republican administration under President George W. Bush in 2001 brought about a significant change in U.S. trade policy vis-à-vis Central America. For one, unlike the Democratic administration that increasingly paid lip service to expanded trade in the Americas during the 1990s,[9] the new Republican government favored free trade as a matter of principle, as was pointed out in the previous chapter. Secondly, the president soon realized Latin America was a key partner in his quest to counterbalance the growing significance of the European Union and the Asia Pacific trading blocks. Yet with recession indicators dominating the U.S. economy throughout 2001, the FTAA negotiations entangled, and internal crises in the larger Latin American markets, one of the best hemispheric options for expanding U.S. markets outside of NAFTA was undoubtedly Central America. This became even more apparent after the terrorist attacks in New York and Washington, when economic considerations became inextricably linked to security concerns.

In early 2002 in a speech before the Organization of American States, President Bush signalled his administration's willingness to consider a free trade negotiation with Central America.[10] The proposed agreement required market liberalization for most goods and services in Central America, including manufacturing, agriculture, government procurement, and public services. The United States promised increased market access in Central America, including textiles and a limited increase in sugar quotas. The agreement proposed to eliminate tariffs on more than 80% of U.S. exports of industrial and consumer products. Reciprocal access would be provided for U.S. products and services. A January 16, 2002, White House press release dryly noted "that close consultations with the U.S. Congress, as well as with leaders in the Central American region" would be required if the initiative were to move forward (Table 4.1).

The would-be signatories to the agreement together represented the second-largest export market in Latin America for U.S. goods and services.

Table 4.1 Excerpts from the White House Announcement on the U.S.–Central American Free Trade Agreement—January 16, 2002

The United States is committed to proceeding with trade initiatives globally, regionally and with individual nations. ... These free trade arrangements will strengthen our economy at home—benefiting American farmers, businesses, workers, and consumers. At the same time, these agreements will promote economic development and democratic governance among our trading partners.

A U.S.–Central America Free Trade Agreement Would:

Promote U.S. Exports: The United States exported $8.8 billion to Central America in 2000 (more than we sold to Russia, Indonesia, and India combined). Mexico and Canada—our NAFTA partners—have already recognized the potential of the Central American market and the need to support Central American reforms by pursuing their own free trade agreements with countries in the region.

The U.S. should not be left behind in North America's economic engagement with Central America. A U.S.–Central America free trade agreement would ensure that American workers and companies are not disadvantaged, build on the $4 billion of U.S. investment in the region, and avoid erosion of U.S. competitiveness.

U.S. duties for the region are already low, as these countries are beneficiaries of the Caribbean Basin Initiative. U.S. imports from Central America totaled $11.8 billion in 2000.

Support Democracy and Economic Reform: during the past decade, Central American countries have established democratic systems of government and begun implementing economic reforms to promote privatization, competition, and open markets.

The proposed free trade agreement with the United States would commit these countries to even greater openness and transparency, which would deepen the roots of democracy, civil society, and the rule of law in the region, as well as reinforce market reforms.

These reforms, coupled with the increased trade and investment flows, would promote expanded growth and openness in the region, as well as support common efforts to achieve stronger environmental protection and improved working conditions.

A free trade agreement would be reciprocal, and without a limited term, unlike current statutory trade preference laws, assuring all partners of a long-term outlook that will strengthen North American cooperation with Central America.

Advance FTAA: this negotiation will complement the United States' goal of completing the Free Trade Area of the Americas (FTAA) no later than January 2005 by increasing the momentum in the hemisphere toward lowering barriers, opening markets, and achieving greater transparency.

The Bush announcement immediately generated an eruption of enthusiasm within the regional business community[11] and provided vindication for the decade-long efforts there to increase trade openness. By the mid-1990s, leaders throughout the region had reduced tariffs unilaterally from an average of 45% in 1985 to around 7% in 2000, among the lowest throughout Latin America.[12]

The U.S. Chamber of Commerce became a major proponent, claiming that a principle benefit of CAFTA would be the elimination of tariffs on substantially all goods and services for U.S. businesses. In Central America the proposal generated significant attention. After many years of unsuccessful attempts to receive the so-called NAFTA parity status under Clinton, the governments of the region were exultant. Costa Rica's Chief Executive Abel Pacheco even proclaimed, "CAFTA will lead us out of poverty."[13] Not surprisingly, in less than a month the presidents of Central America met twice among themselves to draft a regional strategy. They also convened their ministerial and technical teams to follow suit and even rushed to San Salvador to meet President Bush for a few hours at the tail end of his first tour of Latin America. Following a year of hectic negotiations that were held in different U.S. cities and Central American capitals to enhance local support for the agreement, the U.S.–Central American Free Trade Agreement was signed by all parties on August 2004. Given the Dominican Republic's aggressive free trade posture and its earlier commitment to greater Caribbean regional integration efforts, it was invited to join the agreement by its participating neighbors.

Among other benefits, the agreement offered provisions that could be important to sustained market access for the signatories. It would help to consolidate Caribbean Basin Initiative (CBI) access and expand that access to goods that were previously exempted from Central America, while giving reciprocal access for U.S. goods to the signatories. It provided for more flexible rules of origin for textiles and apparel and included reciprocal commitments on access to service markets. Yet, as illustrated below, other dimensions of the agreement engendered an intense response.

Negotiating and signing a multilateral agreement is a difficult undertaking; getting approval in the democratic arenas of each of the signatory countries is quite another. The private and highly structured fora that allow complex agreements to be negotiated are distinct from each countries' more open, pluralistic, noisy, and issue-centric presumably democratic bodies that must debate, argue, and ultimately approve the agreements, as we will illustrate below.

New Battle Lines Formed: The Challenges

Despite the limited impact that the agreement would have on the U.S. economy, the battle lines formed early over the agreement. Central America's devastating conflicts in the 1980s and early 1990s, and its support for U.S. foreign policy in Iraq during the U.S. invasion there in 2003, seem to have been long forgotten as the debate over the agreement picked up steam in the U.S. Congress, proving the point that in the United States "all politics are local." An analysis of the ensuing process suggests a robust intermestic struggle in which the lines between domestic and foreign were definitely blurred.

The debate featured informally and formally organized transnational coalitions, with the single common feature that they did not like some or all components of the trade proposal. The agreement engendered significant opposition from a wide array of social forces within both the United States and Central America. Those opposing the agreement included elected officials, labor unions, agricultural organizations, environmental groups, small and medium-size entrepreneurs, indigenous and women groups, religious entities of different denominations, academics, members of the global-phobic community, and most center–to-left political parties. Because significant CAFTA opponents did not necessarily share a common agenda their demands were seldom expressed in a unitary action platform.

In addition, CAFTA opposition varied in degree and intensity. Some groups rejected the agreement altogether, considering it to be nothing but another tentacle of American imperialism. Other groups, however, advocated renegotiation and have only voiced moderate qualms about specific parts of the current text. Still others, such as the Central American and U.S. Conferences of Roman Catholic Bishops, have come short of denouncing the agreement, voicing support for what they call a "complement" agenda that should be in place to promote the region's development. In their view, this agenda would be indispensable to neutralize the agreement's negative impact upon the most vulnerable sectors of the economy.

The U.S. Congress quickly became a major center of conflict concerning the proposed agreement. Ranking Democrats in the Congress from major U.S. states also campaigned against the agreement.[14] They were critical of the Bush Administration for failing to put together a bipartisan coalition to support the accord. They were unhappy that the agreement did not allow for greater access in Central America to life-saving generic medicines. They were in disagreement about the absence of any effective machinery in the agreement to address internationally recognized labor standards. As a result, they argued, "This CAFTA is on a midnight train to nowhere—in an election year or any year. ..."[15]

They were joined in their opposition to CAFTA by their counterparts from Central America. Legislators from El Salvador argued in part that the agreement encroached upon the country's sovereignty.[16] Deputies of the Honduran Congress linked the impact in Central America with the impact on small businesses in the U.S. by arguing in a letter to the U.S. Congress that "CAFTA is a pre-announced Mitch." They worried that "the negative impacts on the Honduran people will be equal to or worse than the disasters caused by that Hurricane in 1998. We realize that you are not unaware of the future that awaits the Central American and Dominican people under CAFTA, which would equally affect small-scale businesses in the United States."[17] That same year, nine Costa Rican deputies asked the U.S. Congress not to approve the pending agreement, arguing in part that if approved, "in contradiction to national laws, our country could be subject to lawsuits by foreign investors on environmental protection matters." They also warned that the provision to open Internet and cellular telephone services to transnational corporations would deprive the government of necessary funds to provide low-cost services to rural areas and poor urban neighborhoods, thereby "deepening the digital divide" in the country.[18]

Fair traders also found cause to unite around an anti-CAFTA theme. Led by various members of the U.S. Congress, including senior Republican and Democratic senators and congressmen from Florida,[19] they received their major boost from the American Federation of Labor and Congress of Industrial Organizations (AFL-CIO), which argued that CAFTA would not fix Central America's deeply flawed labor laws. A long-time advocate for worker unionization in the region, the labor organization complained that labor "laws fall far below international standards and governments and employers are actively hostile towards unions, [with the result that] this labor chapter model will encourage rampant workers' rights violations to continue. ..." According to the Washington-based labor group, these workers' violations could be found throughout the region. In El Salvador and Nicaragua, workers who were "fired for union organizing have no right to be reinstated." In Guatemala and Honduras, the fines for anti-union discrimination were so low that they did "not effectively deter the practice." In Costa Rica, an International Labor Organization (ILO) recommendation to strengthen remedies for anti-union discrimination had still not been given the force of law.[20]

In the region labor organizations from 18 major federations and confederations from almost all countries demanded stronger workers' rights in CAFTA and pledged to oppose an agreement if it did not include enforceable guarantees for the ILO's core labor standards. While each of these organizations undoubtedly had their independent positions on the agreement, the AFL–CIO served as an important alliance partner for them in their efforts to coalesce the anti-free trade energy and direct it at the U.S. Congress. Thus, in essence, a major nongovernmental organization in the United States used its influence to mobilize and coalesce interests in Central America and the Dominican Republic to oppose a piece of legislation in the U.S. Congress.

Beyond organized labor in and out of the region, other U.S.-based nongovernmental organizations directed their considerable assets toward CAFTA. Public Citizen fashions itself as a national, nonprofit consumer advocacy organization founded to represent consumer interests in Congress, the executive branch, and the courts. Under the leadership of activist Lori Wallach, who directs the Global Trade Watch section of the organization,[21] Public Citizen played a major role in organizing protests in Seattle and played a prominent role in anti-CAFTA efforts.[22] Its anti-CAFTA web site is among the best sources of information on the agreement.[23]

Oxfam has worked with, and supported, leading citizen organizations in the United States, Central America, and South America that advocate for a voice in the formulation of the FTAA. Its general position is that the current international trading system is "rigged to benefit the more powerful and wealthy trading partners." During the CAFTA debate, Oxfam sponsored testimony in Washington by small farmers from the region who argued against CAFTA because it would make it impossible to compete against "highly subsidized" U.S. producers.[24]

In the United States, the League of United Latin American Citizens (LULAC), one of the oldest and most powerful Latino civil rights organizations in the United States, took a strong position against CAFTA, arguing that "like NAFTA, the passage of CAFTA would cause more harm than good by further encouraging the relocation of manufacturing jobs to cheaper labor markets pitting U.S. Latinos and Mexicans against citizens of the global south in a race to the bottom." LULAC also claimed some credit for organizing the grass roots opposition to CAFTA in "labor unions and social organizations in the U.S., Central America, and the Dominican Republic. ..." Together with the Central American Resource Center, the Labor Council for Latin American Advancement and the Salvadoran American National Network, these groups announced on February 8, 2005, their opposition to CAFTA, calling it "exclusionary" and "racist" to Hispanics and Central American natives. They also pointed out that the agreement showed no concern for the negative effects the accord would have on farmers and workers and did not deal with child labor issues.[25]

A final coalition that emerged to oppose CAFTA was organized by environmental groups both within the United States and in the region. U.S.-based groups included the Center for International Environmental Law, Defenders of Wildlife, Earthjustice, Friends of the Earth, the League of Conservation Voters, the National Environmental Trust, the Natural Resources Defense Council, the National Wildlife Federation, the Sierra Club, and the U.S. Public Interest Research Group. They lobbied Congress with three basic messages: that CAFTA's investor rules would undermine U.S. and Central American environmental standards by permitting foreign investors to bypass domestic courts to challenge legitimate laws, that CAFTA's environmental rules did not mandate that any country maintain and enforce basic environmental laws and regulations and they would not ensure that environmental protection in Central America is improved in a meaningful way; and that CAFTA did not ensure food safety and other hygienic standards.[26]

Throughout the region, environmental groups mobilized against the agreement as well.[27] One example that illustrates a full range of concerns can be found in Costa Rica. There the Costa Rican Federation for Environmental Conservation (FECON) railed against the trade agreement, bolstering opposition to it by linking a variety of issues together. The agreement violated the country's sovereignty and undermined its food security. It threatened the livelihoods of thousands of small farmers. The Federation also opposed the likely introduction in the country of transgenetic cotton and soy farms that reflected the interests of multinational agribusiness and that could potentially harm local public health because of allergies and genetic contamination that such products would bring with them.[28]

The Response: Campaigning for CAFTA

Even while the battle lines were forming over the agreement, U.S. and Central American negotiators anticipated key issues: they found a method for exempting the most sensitive products from immediate market introduction. For instance, the United States kept protections for sugar and the textile industry in exchange for long phase-outs of tariffs on Central American dairy, corn, and other farm products such as onions and potatoes.

To convince the U.S. Congress to ratify CAFTA, the Bush administration needed to expend significant political capital. One of the agreement's chief architects, Deputy Secretary of State Robert Zoellick, vigorously campaigned to convince the public affairs community that CAFTA was in the United States' national interest. He acknowledged that "the involvement of the United States in Central America has been episodic, with our attention swinging from intense periods of intervention to long periods of neglect, only to have the region again erupt into our front pages ..." and called attention to the fact that the "domestic debate pays slight attention to the historic opportunity to stabilize and support Central America while promoting America's strategic interests and values."[29] Zoellick's determination in securing ratification of the agreement could also be linked to the continuing delays in negotiating FTAA, the one hemispheric-wide trade agreement that President Clinton had managed to initiate at the 1994 Summit of the Americas in Miami.[30]

For Central America, negotiating a free trade agreement with the United States had its share of difficulties.[31] Panama and the Dominican Republic were latecomers to the process. Costa Rica displayed a great deal of reticence. Countries within the region itself are at different levels of development. These differences placed pressures on the respective countries to protect themselves from giving away too much to the benefit of a neighbor. Differences abounded among the Central American countries in terms of market openness. While El Salvador, Guatemala, and Nicaragua have almost eliminated all state-run utilities through privatization, Costa Rica has not been willing to privatize its insurance and telecommunications state monopolies, claiming that both provide revenue to address strategic needs. Also, of course, several Central American countries are very concerned about agriculture and the impact on small and medium-size producers of basic grains.

Setting aside some of their differences, the Central American presidents campaigned in key U.S. cities in an attempt to neutralize fears that the agreement would weaken the U.S. economy. This increasingly common occurrence, the heads of state of other countries seeking U.S. grass roots support on an issue, is likely to become even more common in the next few decades. Furthermore, CAFTA is already impacting forthcoming Central American presidential campaigns. On June 7, 2005, only two days after being proclaimed a presidential candidate of his party, Oscar Arias—Costa Rican former president and presidential hopeful—traveled to Washington, DC, to lobby in favor of CAFTA in what was widely publicized as his first major campaign act. Interestingly enough, Arias had been preceded by his opponent, Ottón Solís, an outspoken critic of CAFTA. Solís had repeatedly visited Washington, DC, to lobby against the agreement, admittedly using travel funds from anti-CAFTA organizations including Oxfam and the World Friends Committee (the Quakers).

Both Solís and Arias were joined in their Washington errands by the Presidents of Central America and the Dominican Republic, who lobbied U.S. Congressmen in favor of CAFTA. These visits followed separate tours of U.S. cities meant to appease the fears and concerns and bolster the enthusiasm of local business and labor associations.

Hence, gone are the days when Central American presidential candidates would visit their countries' religious shrines in search of blessings and wisdom from above. Today they seem to be besieged by more earthly concerns, many of which cannot be pursued within their nations' own territorial borders or achieved under the benign protection of miraculous saints. Such is the nature of intermestic politics in a post–Cold War world. In all likelihood, it seems that the halls of Congress and the WTO's headquarters in Geneva, not the Basilica of Esquipulas (Guatemala), the Shrine of Suyapa (Honduras), or the Sanctuary of the Virgin of the Angels (Costa Rica), will increasingly be the destination of the political pilgrims of Central America in the years to come.

Ratification Pending and Dilemma Ongoing

In short, ratification and implementation of the agreement became complex matters crossing borders and transcending traditional models of foreign and domestic policy decision-making. The irony is that the region has few good options to attract further foreign investment (and maintain) and even add employment in the face of the growing incidence of Asia and Asian products in the world economy.

A paradox is that Central America could lose with CAFTA, but it could also lose without it. Indeed, with its economy already highly dependent on the U.S. economy (see Chapter 3), the region currently relies on the CBI as an indispensable tool to ensure its competitiveness within it. If the CBI is terminated after the year 2007 (as some lawmakers in Washington and even Bush administration officials have already suggested), and CAFTA is not fully ratified throughout, the region's economies could suffer significant additional stress in gaining access to the United States. If CAFTA were not ratified by the U.S. Congress, and even if the CBI is maintained in its current format, the situation would still remain critical for Central America because of Mexico's advantages *vis-à-vis* Central America in the NAFTA context and the appearance of China as a significant lower-cost producer in the world marketplace.

Yet if CAFTA is ratified (and the CBI comes to an end in due course) and Central America has not been capable of putting together complementary policies and programs that would allow for its most vulnerable social sectors and public institutions to be spared from a projected massive influx of U.S. goods and services, the political impact on the region as a whole or on specific countries could be significant. There has been little political interest in fostering a support of this complementary agenda as a precondition for CAFTA ratification.[32]

In the final analysis these are the reasons why CAFTA has become the ultimate and most vivid example of intermestic politics. It boils down to the core of the national development strategies of all the parties involved. As repeatedly stated by government officials and civil society representatives alike, free trade agreements are not only about enhanced commercial exchange. They involve a wide array of other, even more sensitive issues. Combined, these issues strike at the very essence of the organization of the nation-state and its institutions. Seen in this larger, more complex perspective, CAFTA or any other agreement between a developed nation and its underdeveloped neighbors (particularly if occurring in a context of massive economic and social asymmetries within and between them) produces impacts that cannot, and should not, be measured in trade terms alone.

It is important to consider that trade agreements like CAFTA are capable of altering a small country's long-standing social and political understandings and even reshape its institutions. The negative unintended consequences of such an agreement will be all the more sharply felt if those involved are reluctant to introduce the reforms necessary to ensure that the collateral implications of a totally open market are channeled to the benefit of all the people, not just a small group of (mostly transnational) business interests.

Equally important, unless a well-articulated alternative is found and successfully implemented, the region's poorest would be the first ones to suffer from the closing of trade and investment opportunities if a CAFTA, CBI or their equivalent is not approved. This is particularly the case because of the U.S. weight upon the economy of Central America.

Thus, CAFTA approval presented significant challenges and problems. Central America without CAFTA or an agreement like the CBI faces real dilemmas as well. Unfortunately for the United States and Central America, finding the middle ground has not been possible under the current rules of the game. The signed agreement could only be approved or rejected *in toto* by the parties involved. While minor reforms could be introduced to the text either through explanatory letters that are used to illuminate the meaning of certain provisions or by political agreements made outside of the treaty, the substance of CAFTA could not be modified unless another, almost impossible to imagine, round of negotiations was inaugurated.

By the summer of 2005, the agreement was still pending ratification in the U.S. Congress. Even with the new security environment and even with a strong electoral mandate as a result of his reelection in 2004, President Bush had great difficulty in putting together the votes to secure the support of a Congress dominated by his party in both branches of Congress. If all politics are local in the United States, then the proposed agreement had opened up so many political fronts for the president that clear majority support in the U.S. Congress would be an impossibility. Opposition interests in the United States and in Central America were highly organized and working to stop something that they thought was plainly bad policy. One of the most blatant examples of this is the claim by the U.S. sugar industry that the inclusion of sugar in the agreement could ultimately lead to the destruction of the U.S. sugar industry because it would lead to sugar imports greatly in excess of U.S. needs. Unwilling and unable to ignore the powerful vested interests behind sugar in the United States, the administration ultimately compromised on this matter, hoping to neutralize "Big Sugar's" opposition.

With President Bush directly lobbying many members of his own party in the U.S. House of Representatives, his majority-controlled House barely supported CAFTA through a vote of 217 to 215 in the early morning hours of July 28, 2005. This support, coupled with an earlier positive vote by the U.S. Senate, enabled President Bush to sign CAFTA into law.[33]

In the region the agreement has been ratified by the congresses in Guatemala, El Salvador, Honduras, Panama, and the Dominican Republic. Ratification is still pending in Nicaragua and Costa Rica.

Whatever the impact of CAFTA, though, the negotiations over CAFTA and its ratification in the United States demonstrated once again the small margins of autonomy a subordinate region such as Central America has when dealing with substantive trade and economic factors. These factors tend to be even more powerful and definitive than political ones and are further highlighted by their long-term impact on the people's well-being. Given the dismal human development indices in Central America, the challenge becomes even more daunting. Governments are faced with the dilemma of admitting to the realities and inevitable inequities of the world economy or adopting a firm, albeit largely rhetorical, nationalism that would neither enhance the country's opportunities, nor allow for the protection of its long-term interests. The resolution to this equation will determine improved, mutually beneficial relations between Central America and the United States in the years to come.

CHAPTER 5

Scenarios and Options for the Twenty-First Century: Striving for Relevance in the Global Era

Introduction

The Cold War provided a reliable framework for understanding U.S.–Central American relations for much of the last half of the twentieth century. With the demise of the great power rivalry in the late 1980s, Central America entered into a period of uncertainty as it searched for greater autonomy and freedom in the international system. However, the terrorist attack on the United States in 2001 changed Central America's fortunes again, as a new post–Cold War framework reattached the region directly to U.S. security policy.

This chapter explores several important questions and draws conclusions from the pattern of U.S.–Central American affairs. What are the positive and negative issues that emerged in U.S.–Central American relations in the immediate post–Cold War experience? What lessons for U.S.–Central American affairs come out of the post–9-11 experience? Finally, what is required to bring about a more thoughtful and consistent relationship between the U.S. and Central America?

Positive and Negative Issues in the Immediate
Post–Cold War Experience

The final decade of the twentieth century seemed to have heralded the coming of age of Central America. Unlike other moments in which the region appeared to have been bypassed by history, the closing years of the 1990s allowed Central America to exercise unprecedented leadership in forging its own destiny. The end of the Cold War, the exhaustion in the United States caused by Central American civil strife, and serious U.S. domestic matters relating to economic stagnation gave the region a new moment alone. As a consequence, there was enhanced interest in Central America in the consolidation of democratic politics, the construction of new international alliances, the reexamination of the regional integration system, and the definition of a regional strategy for sustainable human development.

It would be wrong to underestimate the impact these initiatives had in the region at the time. The contending forces in Central America appeared to have learned some bitter lessons of its past. Political elites and their oligarchic backers acknowledged that development could not be achieved in a context dominated by violence and that democracy was irrelevant without adequate levels of economic and social justice for the majorities. However, militant opposition groups realized that prolonged violent conflict was too costly and futile because of the termination of foreign support from Cuba and the Soviet Bloc. In the end, contending groups viewed democracy as an imperfect, yet inevitable, option that could, at the very least, set in place rules of the game that could be accepted by all, including the military.

Freed of the tensions of the Cold War, Central America became more aware of the impact that the new international circumstance had upon its development. Globalization and open markets, competition, and the growing access to information technologies and other knowledge-based processes came as unprecedented opportunities to small nations just becoming untangled from the quagmires of bipolar hostility, misery, and civil war.

Hence, Central America entered the twenty-first century far better off than it entered the twentieth. The region reached unprecedented levels of democracy. For the first time, all the Central American countries are simultaneously ruled by third-generation, democratically elected, civilian presidents. While governance is weak in most countries, the likelihood of a democratic rupture produced by the military is not great, given new forms of civilian control accompanied by hemispheric regulations within the Organization of American States (OAS) and the Summit of the Americas process.

In the economic realm the 1990s witnessed an impressive recovery of countries whose economies had not grown in the previous 25 years. Not even the 1998 devastation produced by Hurricane Mitch in Honduras and Nicaragua was enough to deter regional economic growth that held steady at an impressive 4.5% of gross domestic product throughout the decade.

However, poverty and social exclusion remain the largest and by far the most complicated issues on the regional agenda in the new century. Democratic awakening has not been followed by a decrease in poverty levels. Inequality has risen as a result of macroeconomic reforms and the significant reduction of state-sponsored social investments. While this phenomenon is not exclusive to Central America, it is noteworthy that two of the poorest countries in the Hemisphere, Nicaragua and Honduras, are located in the Isthmus.[1]

Central America's experience during the past two decades should allow the region to draw relevant conclusions for the years to come. The enormous suffering of the 1980s as well as the vulnerable optimism brought about by the 1990s, are assets that the Central American countries have at hand to prevent the repetition of the errors committed in their recent past. Learning the lessons of history could give the region, currently living an unprecedented period of formal democratic governance, an opportunity to eradicate three factors that inhibited the consolidation of the rule of law: violence, impunity, and feeble institutions. Furthermore, they could also help Central America and the United States develop more solid, constructive associations likely to enhance their mutual interests in a globalized economy.

What are some of the lessons learned, and how will they contribute to Central America's democratic consolidation?

Lesson 1: The U.S. will continue to be the preponderant geopolitical force in Central America, but the region will not rank high among U.S. foreign policy priorities.

However, short of major political turmoil or environmental disruption like the one caused by Hurricane Mitch in 1998, Central America will get only limited diplomatic and political attention from the United States. If, and when, CAFTA is finally ratified by all parties, there will be little incentive for the United States to give additional consideration to the isthmus outside the strict limits of its national security strategy or in the larger policy matrix that addresses the hemisphere as a whole, or regions within it, such as NAFTA, MERCOSUR, or the South American Community of Nations. The bad news for Central America, however, is that such hemispheric vision has neither been common nor sustained in U.S. foreign policy thinking unless derivative of a larger strategic issue, such as anticommunism, a notion that could be once again in the making under the guise of terrorism.

Indeed, the successful ratification of the CAFTA will deepen Central American dependency on the U.S. market and investments, mainly because of the region's proximity to the U.S. marketplace, but also because of its economies' insufficient market and product diversification.

Far from forcing Central America into the realities of the new global economy, U.S. predominance has anchored Central American entrepreneurs to the northern markets, whose geographical proximity allows them to neutralize the negative impact of their higher costs of production *vis-à-vis* other, more competitive regions of the world such as China and South East Asia. The growing importance of U.S. dollar remittances in the national economies of El Salvador, Nicaragua, Honduras, and Guatemala further stresses this point.

Lesson 2: Preponderance does not imply submission.

As the Cold War ebbed, Central America demonstrated that it could govern itself and that it was capable of establishing bilateral and multilateral relations outside of direct U.S. influence and control.

The gradual but steady democratization of Central America, the growing complexity of the international arena, and the global nature of issues that compose the bilateral U.S.–Central American agenda, forced the United States to admit, and reluctantly tolerate, this pluralization during the late 1980s and throughout the 1990s. Given U.S. reticence and new budget strategies and priorities that prevented large assistance packages to the region once the peace accords matured, Central America had to look elsewhere for new sources of assistance. This broadening of its international platform enhanced Central American relative autonomy *vis-à-vis* the United States, even as the region stood at the threshold of a new cycle of hegemonic reconstitution.

The political arenas in both Central America and the United States have become more complex in the post–Cold War era largely because of the emergence of nonmilitary or security-related issues and the immediacy of the intermestic agenda. In both regions, parliamentary politics inevitably limit executive branch coherence and autonomy, particularly in relation to trade and foreign policy. The pervasiveness of transnational connections limits state autonomy and further reduces the possibility of policy coherence. As one observer noted, "The particular combination of power and legitimacy we call sovereignty ... is today being partly unbundled, redistributed on other entities and particularly supranational organizations, international agreements on human rights, and the new emergent private international legal regime for business transactions."[2]

As a consequence, the growing complexity of the post–Cold War environment, both domestically and internationally, allowed Central America additional opportunities to expand its relations, but within the traditional context of national interest diplomacy.

Lesson 3: In the post 9-11 environment, the relations between Central America and the United States will develop along the unitarian, state-centric fashion of the past. Yet they will also be increasingly influenced by civil society and other private, nonstate actors that will appear amidst ever-growing intermestic fractures.

Thus, in the first decades of the twenty-first century, the breaking down of traditional alliances and political blocks and the ascension of transnational networks of governmental and nongovernmental actors will continue to impact the U.S.–Central American agenda in ways, and with intensity, unparalleled in the twentieth century. This could take the form of a broad coalition of interests encompassing, for example, parts of what Joel Garreau envisioned as "the nine nations of North America."[3] It is not impossible to imagine, for instance, Central America exploring alliances with Mexico, the Caribbean, and the southern states of the United States, in an attempt to check the "Atlanticist" or even isolationist tendencies of New England, the Northeast "rustbelt," and the midwestern "breadbasket."

Furthermore, free trade, migration and other transnational issues as diverse as organized crime, environmental degradation, the protection of indigenous peoples rights, and social development strategies will help forge unprecedented alliances between U.S. and Central American organizations, official and nongovernmental alike.

The massive pro-immigrant marches throughout the United States in the spring of 2006 protesting new migration legislation revealed the generalized appearance of the national flags of the Central American republics. Still a minority within the ocean of the largely Mexican-born demonstrators, U.S.-based Central American immigrants are becoming increasingly mobilized, vocal, and militant. Salvadoran priests, Guatemalan pastors, and Honduran peasants are now joining hand and hearts in ways never imagined before. These manifestations are indicative of a process of political awakening as much as a proof of cultural affinities above and beyond national origins.

Are U.S.-Central American relations at the threshold of a new age? How will these complex social phenomena express themselves in two or three generations, when and if a U.S. citizen of Central American descent is elected mayor of Washington, DC, or governor of California?

Lesson 4: The end of the Cold War did not bring about the widespread economic and social bonanza necessary to lift the region from its past of deprivation and violence. Regardless of the many positive developments that have taken place in Central America, the fragility of the region remains high.[4]

The conflicts of the 1970s and 1980s ended with a resolution toward more transparent political rules and a broader acceptance of pluralism and democratic governance.[5] This in and of itself was significant, yet major issues remain to be addressed. The region's populations will nearly double within the next 30 years to over 60 million people. While macroeconomic numbers have been improving, per capita income and social investment have not kept pace with the growing demands of the region's population. Hunger is prevalent. Widespread illiteracy impedes productivity. Cross-border and regional migration flourishes, and the brain drain (particularly of knowledge–based workers) continues unabated.[6] Environmental concerns top the regional agenda, while territorial conflicts lingering from the nineteenth century inhibit the possibility of trans-border cooperation strategies in the region's immense binational river basins.[7]

Therefore, while a major crisis like the one that Central America experienced in the late 1970s and 1980s is unlikely to occur in the foreseeable future, significant disruptions—economic, political, and environmental— will continue to threaten regional stability in the decades to come.

The negative agenda that prevailed during the second half of the 1990s impeded the evolution of a more balanced relationship. In the wake of the terrorist attacks of 9-11 and reconstituted U.S. preponderance, the region should seek to prevent a new cycle of security-led pressures that could inhibit the development of a comprehensive agenda, which could be more effectively and thoughtfully addressed by Central America and the United States to the benefit of both.

Lesson 5: U.S. security concerns in Central America, however legitimate, should be addressed within the framework of the region's democratic regimes, upholding the rule of law and seeking to prevent the unnecessary involvement of military institutions in matters not pertaining to national defense.

The democratic awakening of Central America in the 1990s allowed the reframing of civil–military relations. While the armed forces remained a significant political actor, their traditional prerogatives ebbed as the newly elected constitutional civilian authorities took hold of the reigns of government. This positive development was part of a larger trend toward the functional separation of public security and national defense issues, and a necessary step toward the construction of a refurbished, more transparent, and accountable political system built under the aegis of the rule of law. The enactment of the Central American Treaty of Democratic Security in 1995 is the most obvious and positive expression of this unprecedented regional trend that was only stopped by 9-11 concerns.

In Central America only Costa Rica and Panama have been able to eliminate the armed forces as fundamental institutions of their respective state organizations. The existence of professional, nonpartisan, apolitical, and constitutionally obedient armed forces, expensive as this may be, should not be considered incompatible with democracy, even in regions where history has repeatedly proven otherwise.

However, the aggressive engagement of the Central American militaries in development activities in the absence of consolidated national institutions could put the region at the threshold of a new cycle of undesirable military interventionism, particularly given the growing role of the military in domestic security and antiterrorism matters. In the context of the region's history of civil–military relations, this could only bring about unnecessary tensions that could deteriorate into dangerous authoritarian scenarios.

Hence, it is important that the United States and its Central American counterparts find creative ways to address their common and legitimate security concerns within the framework of the rule of law and without threatening the still-fragile civilian authority over the military.

Lesson 6: Leadership counts.

Latin Americans often blame the United States for most of their problems, historical or recent, political, military, or socioeconomic. While there are sufficient grounds to sustain that accusation, they themselves can be held accountable for some of the region's most significant difficulties. Either through political mismanagement, ethical wrongdoing, or sheer lack of vision, Latin American elites cannot neglect their share of responsibility for their countries' well-being.

The history of Central America during the 1990s shows that leadership, if exercised correctly, can, and does, make a difference. When Central American leaders have been able to put together a creative, united proposal, their voices have been heard, even in the generally distant hallways of Congress or the White House. True, those proposals also required an auspicious context in which to develop, be it international (such as the end of the Cold War) or domestic (the democratic dawn in Central America or the growing awareness of and impinging regional crisis due to U.S. mismanagement, for instance). Yet when the leaders of Central America are capable of putting forward a vision, the United States tends to be more receptive, or at least less prone to act with its usual hegemonic demeanor.

There is an old, well-proven fact in politics: there are no empty spaces. Central America should learn a corollary to that thesis: if the vacuum is not empty, then it doesn't need to be filled.

As Central America matured and its political systems became stronger and more institutionalized during the 1990s, the United States expected greater levels of regional stability and consolidation. Unfortunately, the seemingly undisputed recognition by the Central American presidents (as expressed in adoption of ALIDES in 1994) that in the current age, true development entails first and foremost a commitment from each country to assume the costs of human development, did not come to fruition. Much to the despair of civil society in the region, it soon became obvious that Central America's elites were not quite ready to give up the historical prerogatives they had exercised at the expense of the poor in their countries. In addition, the dominant structures of power were not ready to withstand and incorporate the demands of a newly democratized region into the decision-making process.

It is still possible to reverse this trend. In order to do it, though, Central America's leaders must recreate the regional networks and political dialogue that their predecessors put to the test during the Esquipulas negotiations or in the early 1990s, when they were able to bring forth ALIDES and other significant openings to the world. Otherwise, preponderance and a true lack of stimulus on the part of the United States will continue to curtail Central America's opportunities to partake in the construction of a new, vibrant hemispheric community.

What is Required to Bring about a More Thoughtful Relationship between the United States and Central America?

Given this very complex framework, how can the United States and Central America forge a constructive relationship in the next decades? It is necessary to make a mature assessment of the areas of convergence and divergence and how they will be addressed in the mid and long terms. This assessment cannot and should not ignore the significant asymmetries between the areas or the realities imposed on the relationship by the new international threats and the inevitable, bold, and often unilateral U.S. responses to them. Nonetheless, it should also acknowledge the new conditions that pervade Central America in the post–Cold War era, particularly the emergence of democratic regimes whose legitimacy should not be taken for granted.

As long as the United States considers Central America solely as a source of environmental, human, or political threats rather than as a partner with whom to confront common (not only security-related) challenges, the possibility to overcome the preeminence of this negative agenda is bleak. Finding common ground requires the recognition of mutual grievances, but most importantly, it also presumes the willingness to address them jointly in a constructive and effective manner.

Few will dispute the legitimacy of many of the negative issues that concern the United States with respect to Central America. Drug trafficking, illegal immigration, economic and social dumping, the devastation of the environment, or even the unlikely scenario of Central America becoming a nest of terrorists disguised as undocumented migrants who could creep into the United States are issues that either affect the United States or have an impact on its global outlook. It is equally true, nevertheless, that Central America has legitimate concerns—trade access, poverty, inequality, and immigration policy—that the United States should not ignore or overlook because they bear a very heavy burden upon the region's future development.

The signing of CONCA–USA in 1994 was a step in the right direction. For the first time, the United States and Central America were able to identify a substantive list of mutual concerns in the environmental realm and define a common strategy to address them. Similarly, the decision by President Clinton and his Central American counterparts to start rounds of periodic consultations to address specific areas of common interest was an important contribution to the definition of this new agenda resulting from dialogue and mutual understanding. President Bush's determination to seek and get the approval of CAFTA was yet another indication that it is possible and desirable to find areas in which the United States and Central America can find a sense of purpose above and beyond narrow national or sectoral interests.

Yet the high expectations brought about by some of these unprecedented agreements were not justified, given the absence of subsequent follow-up. Other agreements have proven insufficient to meet the larger, more complex challenges arising from decades of political neglect and social injustice.

In an age of reconstituted predominance, for example, it could be desirable for Central America and the United States to forge a more institutionalized relationship that could take place in the wider context of the North American framework that has been painstakingly built by the United States with its NAFTA partners, Mexico and Canada. After all, Central America already has trade and political agreements with Mexico and Canada. They have also developed a long-standing relationship with Mexico through the so-called Tuxtla Dialogue.[8] While Central America could not possibly match either Canada's or Mexico's strategic importance to the United States, the possibility of its joining the northern triangle could bolster a new sense of regional partnership beyond the strict limits of free trade considerations.

In this regard, given their reduced strategic relevance, Central America and the Caribbean could probably generate greater attention from the United States if they perfect their integration mechanisms or at least form a political and economic association, loose and informal as it may be. This would entail the defeat of long-standing cultural barriers that have prevented a fruitful relationship between the two regions and the advent of a vision of the Greater Caribbean as a driving force of democratic and economic stability in the northern part of the hemisphere. An essential part of the equation would be the incorporation of Cuba, for it is inconceivable to isolate the largest insular state of the Caribbean from the overall development of the region.

Kenichi Omae has proposed the end of the nation-state and its substitution with what he calls the "city region."[9] According to Omae, the dynamics of the world economy are rendering the state incapable of its traditional role as arbiter of national communities. In his view, bureaucratic fragmentation and regionalism also contribute significantly to the demise of the nation-state. The growth of metropolises with enough economic power and derived political clout allows them to become alternative poles of development. Thus, a new power balance is established, determined not so much by geographic boundaries or ethnicity, as by the capacity of those megacities to deliver benefits to the populations within their areas of influence regardless of their ethnic or national origins.

Omae's prediction could be a compelling scenario for a completely new relationship between Central America and the United States in the twenty-first century. It is possible to find some elements that could eventually bring about a city-region in the Caribbean Basin. Many U.S. cities are the largest conglomerates of some national groups (lessening their territorial linkage to their countries of origin). Also, certain cities have become the financial and entrepreneurial centers of the Greater Caribbean. In a fully interconnected world, it would not be difficult to imagine Miami becoming the epicenter of a Greater Caribbean Community whose national borders had been erased by the invisible webs of the Internet.

This network of regions encompassing parts of the United States, Mexico, Colombia, Venezuela, the member states of SICA, CARICOM, Cuba, and the Dominican Republic has already started to take shape. In 1993 all these countries, with the exception of the United States, created the Association of Caribbean States. This subregional institution remains weak and unfocused and lacks the political relevance necessary to become the true hub of a Greater Caribbean Community in the short term. Yet its appearance is more than symbolic. It depicts the recognition of a supranational reality that clearly does not stem from cultural, ethnic, or even ideological affinity, but rather from geopolitical commonality. It also heralds the coming about of an unprecedented effort to initiate cooperation among the Spanish- and English-speaking countries of Central America and the Caribbean.[10]

While any such arrangement may still lie decades away, the state-centered relationship between the Central American republics and the United States will continue to experience important transformations as the twenty-first century matures. The majority of those changes will most likely be related to economic and technological change. It would be impossible, however, not to imagine political factors becoming increasingly significant, particularly if democracy is challenged by growing social discontent in the isthmus and the United States struggles to maintain its global predominance in the international system.

U.S. and Central American leaders will be forced to make a strategic decision sooner rather than later. Facing increasing economic competition and new political dilemmas, they will have to become either true partners (asymmetrical as that partnership may be) on a joint, regional, long-term strategy or surrender to the traditional historical forces and remain separated by a pervasive wall of unilateral impositions and unfulfilled expectations.

Realists in the United States and Central America would quickly argue that neither scenario entails any fundamental difference for the regional hegemon or its subordinate ally. After all, the United States will always carry the bigger part of the load as Central America continues to struggle for political stability and economic development. Moreover, they will correctly assume that deprived of any credible threat in the area, the United States could very well manage new crises in Central America (even large ones) without having to contest, as was the case during the Cold War, the unfriendly advances of any major global competitors.

It is true that in the large picture of world politics, Central America is not likely to become a principal concern of the United States, particularly on the heels of 9-11. Nor is Central America ever likely to enjoy the prominence of the larger Latin American nations, with the obvious exception of Mexico, the United States' immediate neighbor and most important trading partner. Similarly, it would be naïve to suggest that Central America could become an interlocutor on equal footing with the United States in whatever form of association it chooses to form in this new millennium.

Yet, as the events in the 1980s and 1990s proved, an unstable and violent Central America could cause significant havoc in domestic U.S. politics, especially if that instability and violence is accompanied by large population displacements and enduring economic deprivation. Such a scenario would be even more difficult if it were to occur in a Latin American context dominated by nationalistic and even anti-U.S. governments such as the ones that have been elected in Venezuela, the Andean Region, or even closer, in Mexico and Nicaragua.

The question therefore should not be whether the vital national security interests of the United States would in any way be threatened or compromised by events in twenty-first century Central America. Short of an apocalyptic tragedy, nothing that could be anticipated in the foreseeable future could do so. Rather, the real issue at stake concerns what way would it be easier, more effective, and less costly for Central America and the United States to bear the realities of their geopolitical proximity. Clearly, those challenges would be better addressed in an amicable, cooperative, and economically sound context within the framework of functioning and governable democratic regimes.

Endnotes

Introduction

1. See, for instance, "The World Ahead," *Foreign Affairs*, Vol. 76, No. 5, September/October 1997; "What Comes after the 'Post–Cold War World,'" *Foreign Policy*, No. 119, Summer 2000.
2. For his part, British Prime Minister Winston Churchill, speaking in Missouri earlier in 1946, warned that "… an Iron Curtain had descended across the continent," galvanizing a world-view that dominated U.S. foreign policy until the collapse of the Berlin Wall in 1989.
3. See Peter Trubowitz, *Defining the National Interest: Conflict and Change in American Foreign Policy*. Chicago: University of Chicago Press, 1998, pp. 237–238.
4. Samuel P. Huntington, "The Erosion of American National Interests," *Foreign Affairs*, September/October 1997.
5. Thomas L. Friedman, *The World Is Flat: A Brief History of the Twenty First Century*. New York: Farrar, Strauss and Giroux, 2005.
6. Michael Mazarr, ed., *Information Technology and World Politics*. New York: Palgrave MacMillan, 2002.
7. Robert D. Kaplan, "Supremacy by Stealth," *The Atlantic Monthly*, July–August 2003, p. 2.
8. Immanuel Wallerstein, *After Liberalism*, New York: New Press. p. 25; See also James Rosenau, "Patterned Chaos in Global Life: Structure and Process in the Two Worlds of World Politics," *International Political Science Review*, Vol. 4, No. 9, Winter 1988, pp. 327–64; James Rosenau, "A Pre-Theory Revisited: World Politics in an Era of Cascading Interdependence," *International Studies Quarterly*, Vol. 28, Summer 1984, pp. 245–305.
9. José Manuel Salazar, "Las asimetrías en los TLC contemporáneos y el TLC Centroamérica-EEUU (CAFTA)," San José: Academia de Centroamérica, 2003.
10. The National Security Strategy of the United States, September 2002, p. 5.

11. See Attorney General John Ashcroft, "Preserving Life and Liberty," a speech before law enforcement officers in Boise, Idaho, August 25, 2003, in Thomas E. Baker and John F. Stack, Jr. *At War with Civil Rights and Civil Liberties*, Oxford: Rowman & Littlefield, 2006, p. 17–24.
12. See Juan Manuel Villasuso and Rafael Trejos Solorzano, eds., *Comercio e integración en las Américas*, San José: BID, INTAL, UCR, IIE: IICA, 1999.
13. Mesoamerica is the region occupied by southern Mexico and the Yucatan, all of Belize, Guatemala, El Salvador, Honduras, Nicaragua, Costa Rica, and Panama. Collectively, their inhabitants are known as Mesoamericans and they share cultural traits. These include hieroglyphic writing, screen-fold books, masonry ball courts, interest and knowledge of astronomy and mathematics, three calendars, and a common pantheon of gods, goddesses, and monsters. Common cultural traits also include a diet based on corn, beans, and squash, which is still very much alive in Mexico and Central America.

Chapter 1

1. Walter LaFeber, *Inevitable Revolutions: The United States in Central America*, New York: WW Norton, 1983; John H. Coatsworth, *Central America and the United States: The Clients and the Colossus*, New York: Twayne, 1994; Mark T. Gilderhus, *The Second Century: US-Latin American Relations since 1889*, Wilmington: SR Books, 2000.
2. This characteristic has been analyzed by Christopher Layne, "Rethinking American Grand Strategy: Hegemony or Balance of Power in the Twenty-first Century," *World Policy Journal*, Summer, 1998. Also Michael Elliot, *The Day Before Yesterday*, New York: Simon & Schuster, 1996.
3. Francisco Rojas and Luis G. *Solís, Súbditos o Aliados? La política exterior de los EEUU y Centroamérica*, San José: Porvenir, 1988.
4. Lars Schoultz, *Beneath the United States: A History of U.S. Policy Towards Latin America*, Boston: Harvard University Press, 1998.
5. John Ruggie, *Winning the Peace*, New York: Columbia University Press, 1996;
6. Quoted in Michael Minkenberg and Herbert Dittgen, eds., *The American Impasse: US Domestic and Foreign Policy after the Cold War*, Pittsburgh: University of Pittsburgh Press, 1996, p. xvii.
7. Samuel Huntington, "The Erosion of American National Interests," *Foreign Affairs*, September–October 1997, Vol. 76, p. 28.
8. These treaties, gradually implemented through almost a quarter of a century, allowed Panama to regain full control of the Canal and its adjacent areas on December 31, 1999.
9. Ronald Reagan, State of the Union Address, February 6, 1985.
10. Idem.
11. The so-called Iran-Contra scandal resulted from the disclosure of illegal activities performed by high- and mid-level functionaries of the White House and the U.S. National Security Council in association with foreign private agents. Basically, these actions entailed significant transfers of funds and weapons to the government of Iran in exchange for the release of American hostages. Part of those funds were later channeled to the U.S.-backed

Nicaraguan rebels without Congressional authorization. The scandal was investigated by the Tower Commission and resulted in the indictment of several functionaries. While significant suspicion existed of President Reagan's knowledge of the affair, the Tower Commission was never able to prove it.

12. The Esquipulas Peace Plan, also known as the Arias Peace Plan or the Central American Peace Plan, was signed in Guatemala on August 7, 1987. Originally proposed by Costa Rican President Oscar Arias, who was awarded the Nobel Peace Prize for his efforts, it was later adopted by the other Central American Presidents and became the foundation for the regional agreements that put an end to the internal conflicts in Nicaragua (1990), El Salvador (1992), and Guatemala (1996).

13. The Monroe Doctrine was expressed during President Monroe's seventh annual message to Congress, December 2, 1823, in the following terms: "At the proposal of the Russian Imperial Government, made through the minister of the Emperor residing here, a full power and instructions have been transmitted to the minister of the United States at St. Petersburg to arrange by amicable negotiation the respective rights and interests of the two nations on the northwest coast of this continent. A similar proposal has been made by His Imperial Majesty to the Government of Great Britain, which has likewise been acceded to. The Government of the United States has been desirous by this friendly proceeding of manifesting the great value that they have invariably attached to the friendship of the Emperor and their solicitude to cultivate the best understanding with his Government. *In the discussions to which this interest has given rise and in the arrangements by which they may terminate the occasion has been judged proper for asserting, as a principle in which the rights and interests of the United States are involved, that the American continents, by the free and independent condition which they have assumed and maintain, are henceforth not to be considered as subjects for future colonization by any European powers....*" University of Oklahoma Law Center Online. Available at http://www.Law.Ou.Edu/Hist/Monroedoc. html. For information on U.S. threat perceptions during the early Reagan presidency, see Alexander Haig, *Caveat Realism*, London: Weidenfelt & Nicolson 1984.

14. Luis G. Solis, "Collective Mediations in the Caribbean Basin," in *Collective Responses to Regional Problems: The Case of Latin America and the Caribbean*, edited by Carl Kaysen, Robert A. Pastor, and Laura W. Reed, Cambridge: American Academy of Arts and Sciences, 1994.

15. See Charles D. Brockett, Political Movements and Violence in *Central America*, Cambridge: Cambridge University Press, 2005.

16. Rodolfo Cerdas, *La Hoz y el Machete*, San José, Costa Rica: UNED, 1989.

17. Vladimir de la Cruz, *La Reforma Social*, San José: Editorial Costa Rica, 1974.

18. Jacobo Schifter, *La Fase Oculta de la Guerra Civil en Costa Rica (Colección Seis)*, San Jose, Costa Rica: Editorial Universitaria Centroamericana, 1979; Stephen C. Schlesinger, and Stephen Kinzer, *Bitter Fruit: The Story of the American Coup in Guatemala*, Cambridge, MA: Harvard University Press, 1999; Cole Blasier, *The Hovering Giant*, Pittsburgh, PA: The University of Pittsburgh Press, 1979; John Patrick Bell, *Guerra Civil en Costa Rica: Los Sucesos Políticos de 1948*, 2nd ed, Costa Rica: Trejos Hnos, 1981.

19. Walt W. Rostow, *Economics of Take Off into Sustained Growth*, London: Palgrave MacMillan, 1969.
20. Walter LaFeber, *Inevitable Revolutions*, New York: W.W. Norton, 1993.
21. The National Security Doctrine was originally proposed by President John F. Kennedy as a U.S. response to Soviet Communism in the 1960s. Among other issues, it called for enhanced intelligence activities within the U.S. military missions abroad and fomented and supported the involvement of the armed forces of its allies in domestic security duties to curtail "Communist aggression." The led to some of the most serious human rights violations in Central America and South East Asia.
22. Robert Pastor, *Condemned to Repetition,* Princeton, N.J.: Princeton University Press, 1989.
23. Samuel Stone, *The Heritage of the Conquistadors*, Lincoln, Nebraska: University of Nebraska Press, 1991.
24. Kevin Casas and Arnoldo Brenes, *Los Militares como Empresarios*, San José, Costa Rica: Fundación Arias, 1998.
25. Furthermore, regardless of this suspension, repeatedly breached during the Reagan and Bush Administrations, the final report of the Guatemala National Commission for Historic Truth demonstrated how the military and paramilitary organizations murdered more than 150,000 peasants, mostly indigenous, in less than two decades. Also see Robert Pastor, *Exiting the Whirlpool: U.S. Foreign Policy Toward Latin America and the Caribbean*, Boulder, CO: Westview Press, 2001.
26. Darío Moreno, *U.S. Policy in Central America: The Endless Debate*, Miami: FIU, 1990.
27. W. Frick Curry, Altered States: Post–Cold War U.S. Security Interests in Central America, a report by the Center for International Policy, Washington, DC, 1995.
28. Congress of the United States, Support to the Contadora Process: A Report of the Committee of Foreign Affairs of the U.S. House of Representatives (H.Congr.Res.283), Washington, DC. Also see Bruce Bagley, *Contadora and the Diplomacy of Peace in Central America*, Boulder, CO: Westview Press, 1987.
29. Luis G. Solis, "Collective Mediations in the Caribbean Basin," 1995. A firsthand, less critical perspective can be found in Robert Pastor, *Exiting The Whirlpool: U.S. Foreign Policy Toward Latin America and The Caribbean*, Boulder, CO: Westview Press, 2001.
30. Henry A. Kissinger, "American Foreign Policy: Problems and Opportunities," speech delivered on April 16, 1984, at the Commonwealth Club. Available at http://www.commonwealthclub.or/archive/84/84-04-04kissinger-speech.html.
31. John D. Martz et al., *United States Policy in Latin America: A Quarter Century of Crisis and Challenge*, (reprint) Lincoln, Nebraska: University of Nebraska Press, 1990.
32. John A. Booth and Thomas W. Walker, *Understanding Central America*, Boulder, CO: Westview Press, 1989.
33. Alicia Frohmann, *Puentes Sobre la Turbulencia*, Santiago, Chile: FLACSO, 1988.

34. Johanna Oliver, "The Esquipulas Process: A Central American Paradigm for Resolving Regional Conflict," *Ethnic Studies Report*, Vol. XVII, No. 2, July 1999.
35. U.S. Department of State, Negotiations in Central America (1981–1987), Washington, DC, 1987.
36. John Peeler, "Central America and the United States: Cycles of Containment and Response," in John D. Martz, *United States Policy in Latin America: A Decade of Crisis and Challenge,* Lincoln, Nebraska: The University of Nebraska Press, 1995.
37. The Nicaraguan government and all the parties of the opposition requested the United States to suspend aid to the rebels during the presidential summit of Tela, Honduras, in late 1988. This petition, endorsed by the other countries of the region, was part of the measures negotiated by the Nicaraguan leaders to carry out new presidential elections in February of 1990. The United States declined, and the support was continued through 1989 amidst a furious debate in the U.S. Congress. In the 1990 elections, Daniel Ortega, the incumbent president, was defeated by Violeta Barrios, thus ending a decade-long rule by the Sandinista party.
38. See the excellent article by Steve C. Ropp, "The Bush Administration and the Invasion of Panama: Explaining the Choice and Timing of the Military Option," in John D. Martz, ed. *US Policy in Latin America: A Decade of Crisis and Change,* Lincoln, Nebraska: University of Nebraska Press, 1995.
39. Margaret Scranton, *The Noriega Years: The U.S.-Panamanian Relations* 1981–1990, Boulder, CO: Lynne Rienner, 1991.
40. John Dinges, *Our Man in Panama*, New York: Random House, 1990.
41. Frederick Kempe, *Divorcing the Dictator,* New York: G.B. Putham's Sons, 1990. The high priority of drugs as a major national threat to the United States has been kept. See George A. Joulwan, CINC U.S. Southern Command, Statement before the Senate Committee con Foreign Relations, Subcommittee on Terrorism, Narcotics and International Operations, Prepared Statement for the U.S. Senate Committee on Armed Services hearings, 103 Congress, 2nd session. April 22, 1994.

Chapter 2

1. Henry A. Kissinger, *Does America need a Foreign Policy?,* New York: Simon and Schuster, 2002. For conflicting views on these challenges, see Joseph Nye, *The Paradox of American Power*, New York: Oxford University Press, 2002 and John J. Mearsheimer, *The Tragedy of Great Power Politics*, New York: W.W. Norton, 2001.
2. See Mark B. Rosenberg, ed., T*he Changing Hemispheric Trade Environment,* Miami: Florida International University, 1991.
3. Roberto Herrera Cáceres, *El Libro Blanco de Centroamérica*, San Salvador: SG-SICA, 1998. Also see Victor Bulmer-Thomas, *Centroamérica en Reestructuración: Integración Regional en Centroamérica,* San Jose, Costa Rica: FLACSO-SSRC, 1998. A more prospective view can be found in Luis G. Solis, *Centroamérica 2020: La Integración Regional y el Desafío de sus Relaciones Externas*, Hamburgo: Instituto de Estudios Latinoamericanos, 2002.

4. A strong critique of the current model of Central American integration can be found in Rodolfo Cerdas, *Las Instituciones de Integración en Centroamérica: De la Retórica a la Descomposición*, San José, Costa Rica: EUNED, 2005.

5. One analyst has noted that "we became complacent during the 1990's"; see Joseph Nye, *The Paradox of American Power*, New York: Oxford University Press, 2002, p. ix.

6. Jean-Bertrand de la Grange and Maite Rico, *Marcos: La Genial Impostura*, Madrid: Aguilar/Santillana, 1999.

7. See John D. Martz, ed., *United States Policy in Latin America: A Decade of Crisis and Challenge*, Lincoln: University of Nebraska Press, 1995.

8. Luis G. Solís, *Quién es Quien?*, San José, Costa Rica: 1998.

9. William L. Furlong, "David y Goliath: Relaciones entre Estados Unidos y Costa Rica en el Periodo de la Posguerra Fría," *Revista Relaciones Internacionales*, No. 54, Primer Semestre 1996, Heredia: EUNA, pp.13–24.

10. Tower Commission Report (Report of the President's Special Review Board). Washington, D.C.: U.S. Government Printing Office, 1989.

11. "Think Again: Clinton's Foreign Policy," Foreign Policy, November/December 2000, pp. 18–20.

12. Gonzalo J. Facio, *Litigando en Washington*, Heredia: UNA, 1995.

13. Joseph Thompson, "Costa Rica y los Estados Unidos," in Fernando Naranjo and Luis Guillermo Solís, eds., *Paz, Integración y Desarrollo: La Política Exterior de Costa Rica 1994–1998*, San José, Costa Rica: EUNA, 1999.

14. Cumbre Ecológica de Nicaragua, *Declaración del Volcán Masaya*, Managua: October 12, 1994.

15. The final text of CONCA–USA has two well-defined parts: a political declaration and a plan of action. The first part begins with a reference to an issue in which no agreement was reached: trade. Immediately after this, the United States accepts the Central American invitation to become the "first extra-regional partner of ALIDES" followed by the environmental issues that will be jointly addressed by the parties. The four environmental priorities identified were the efficient use of clean energy, the preservation and rational use of biodiversity, the strengthening of environmental laws, and the harmonization of environmental standards. The agreement was to be reviewed on a periodic basis by the specialized agencies in charge of the issues. The text allowed the parties to include new topics of mutual interest in the agreement. The Action Plan was divided into four parts, one for each of the theme priorities. Interestingly enough, it was in this operational part of the declaration that the United States agreed to "… press as vigorously as possible and as soon as the Congress is in session next January, to obtain the approval of the Interim Trade Program." This was never accomplished.

16. Consultores Económicos y Financieros S.A. (CEFSA), *El Huracán Mitch y su Impacto Económico en Centroamérica*, San José, Costa Rica, Enero, 1999.

17. "Despair could spark immigration," *The Miami Herald*, November 20, 1998.

18. The White House Briefing Room, "President Clinton's Relief Assistance for Central America," December 11, 1998.

19. Rep. Cass Ballenger, Hearing before the Subcommittee on International Relations, House of Representatives, 105th Congress, June 25, 1997.

20. William Branigin, "US Admits Wave of Illegal Migrants Fleeing Mitch's Wake," *The Washington Post,* February 8, 1998.
21. Bill Clinton, Speech in Posoltega, Nicaragua, March 8, 1999.
22. U.S. Department of State, *On-the-record-briefing by Wendy Sherman, State Department Counselor and Mark Schneider, USAID Assistant Administrator for Latin American and the Caribbean,* Washington, DC, January 28, 1999.
23. See Transparency International's index found at http://www.transparency. org/tilac/indices/indices_percepcion/1998/1998.ipc.html.
24. "Republicanos Piden Control," *La Nación,* March 10, 1999. "Pugna en EEUU por Ayuda al Istmo," *La Nación,* March 19, 1999. "Debate Atrapa Ayuda al Istmo," in *La Nación,* April 16, 1999.
25. U.S. Secretary of Commerce William Daly quoted by Rosa Towsend, "EEUU Sugiere a Centroamérica que se Olvide de Entrar en el TLC," *El País,* February 5, 1999.
26. "Cumbre con Clinton deja Insatisfechos a los Centroamericanos," *Agence France Press,* March 12, 1999.
27. "Calderón: Es Hora de Exigir Más Comercio y Mejor Trato a Inmigrantes," *Agence France Press,* March 9, 1999.
28. Manuel Orozco, "Distant Brothers," *Hemisphere,* 8(3): 30–36, 1998.
29. The group included Vice President Richard Cheney, Secretary of Defense Ronald Rumsfeld, Deputy Defense Secretary Paul Wolfowicz, National Security Advisor Condoleezza Rice, U.S. Trade Representative Robert Zoellick, and former Department of State high-ranking officers such as Elliot Abrams, Roger Noriega, Otto Reich, and John Negroponte.
30. George W. Bush speech on Latin America, delivered at a campaign rally at Florida International University on August 25, 2000.
31. Gamarra, Eduardo, "From the Editor," *Hemisphere,* 14:3 2004.

Chapter 3

1. Michael Hirsh, "Bush and the World," *Foreign Affairs,* September/October: 18–19, 2002.
2. Remarks to the Council of the Americas, Washington, DC, May 3, 2005.
3. See Victor Bulmer-Thomas and A. Douglas Kincaid, *Central America 2020: Towards a New Regional Development Model, Hamburg Institute for Iberoamerican Studies, 2000* and "Security Collaboration and Confidence Building in the Americas," in Jorge I. Domínguez, ed., *International Security and Democracy: Latin America and the Caribbean in the Post–Cold War Era,* Pittsburgh, PA: Pittsburgh University Press, 1998.
4. See "Caribbean Geopolitics and Geonarcotics: New Dynamics, Same Old Dilemma," *Naval War Collage Review,* 51(2) (Spring): 47–67, 1998; "U.S. Strategic Interests in Caribbean Security," Joint Force Quarterly, 25 (Autumn): 64–69, 2000; *Drugs and Security in the Caribbean: Sovereignty Under Siege,* University Park: Pennsylvania State University Press, 1997; "The Decentralization Imperative and Caribbean Criminal Enterprises," in Tom Farer ed., *Transnational Crime in the Americas,* New York: Routledge, 1999, 143–170; "The Caribbean in a New Strategic Environment," in Joseph S. Tulchin and Francisco Rojas Aravena, eds., *Strategic Balance and Confidence Building Measures in the Americas,* Stanford: Stanford University Press, 1998.

5. Gabriel Aguilera, "La Espada Solidaria. Cooperación en Seguridad y Defensa en Centroamérica," ponencia en el Taller sobre Seguridad, Defensa y Cooperación en las Américas, Santiago de Chile, April 1998.

6. Institute for National Strategic Studies, "Nuevos Modelos para la Seguridad Cooperativa entre los Paises de Centroamérica," in *Strategic Forum*, No. 17, January 1995; Francisco Rojas Aravena, ed., *Peace, Regional Crisis and US Foreign Policy*, Santiago, Chile: FLACSO, 2003; Monica Hirst, "Los Claroscuros de la Seguridad Regional en las Américas," *Nueva Sociedad*, 185 (May–June):83–101 2003.

7. Jerry Haar and Bryan Anthony, eds., *Canadian-Caribbean Relations in Transition: Trade, Sustainable Development and Security*, London: Palgrave/MacMillan, 1999.

8. U.S. Department of Defense, *United States Strategy for the Americas*, Washington, DC: Office of International Security Affairs, 1995; Maria Cristina Rosas, ed., *Seguridad Hemisférica: Un Largo y Sinuoso Camino*, Mexico: UNAM, 2003, especially the chapter by Rosas, "Existe la Seguridad Hemisférica?," pp. 30–74.

9. The data used in this and the following sections to describe current developments in Central America are drawn from a 2003–2005 review of selected information published by this region's most important newspapers. The authors express their appreciation to the Central American Foundation for Peace and Democracy (FUNPADEM) for its willingness to provide access to this important collection.

10. As of May 2005, a contingent of 350 Salvadoran soldiers remains as the sole contribution of Central America to the U.S. dominated coalition in Iraq. The Honduras and Nicaraguan troops were recalled once the newly elected Socialist government of Spain decided to withdraw its Plus Ultra Battalion after the March 11, 2003, terrorist attack in Madrid. The government of Costa Rica was forced to abandon the Coalition of the Willing by a Supreme Court ruling that explicitly forbade the executive branch from participating in any way in an armed conflict without an explicit authorization from the Legislative Assembly, Costa Rica's congress. Since then, El Salvador has undoubtedly become the United States' closest and most reliable ally in the region by virtue of its steadfast military support to the United States in Iraq.

11. This was witnessed and underwritten by U.S. Undersecretary of Defense Dan Fisk, who was present in Tegucigalpa as a guest of honor at the time.

12. See "Patriot Act Redux and in the Dark," *The New York Times* (editorial), June 1, 2005, p. A-22.

13. See "Informe-Resumen, Latinobarómetro 2004: Una Década de Mediciones," *Santiago: Corporación Latinobarometro*, 2004, www.latinobarometro.org.

14. Remarks before the Council of the Americas, Washington, DC, May 3, 2005.

15. Examples abound. As of 2005, three Central American former presidents (Nicaragua's Alemán and Costa Rica's Calderón and Rodríguez) were in prison or awaiting trial. Another one (Guatemala's Portillo) fled to Mexico after the discovery of his presumed involvement in monumental frauds and other financial wrongdoings. Former Panamanian President Moscoso, currently immune owing to her membership in the Central American Parliament she once despised as "Ali Baba's cave," is also being questioned for massive unaccounted for or unjustified expenses during her term in office.

16. These gangs are not to be confused with the so-called *maras*, juvenile criminal organizations whose origins and current doings will be analyzed later in this chapter.

17. According to the CSIS, as quoted by Luis Fernando Ayerbe in his excellent article "Percepcoes Norte-Americanas Sobre os Impasses na America Latina," in Gilberto Dupas, ed., America Latina no Inicio do Seculo XXI, Rio de Janeiro/Sao Paulo: KAS/UNESP, 2004, p. 2006.

18. As reflected in the annual reports of the Bureau for International Narcotics and Law Enforcement Affairs (The International Narcotics Control Strategy Report) and the Executive Policy Summary of the National Drug Intelligence Center.

19. Federal Bureau of Investigations, *The FBI's Counterterrorism Program*, Washington, DC: The National Commission on Terrorist Attacks upon the United States, April, 2004.

20. According to Michael J. Garcia, Assistant Secretary of U.S. Immigration and Customs Enforcement, based on intelligence assessments, as of 2005 the "Mara Salvatrucha" poses the greatest threats in Los Angeles, New York, Miami, Baltimore, Newark, and Washington DC; Hearing on "Immigration and the Alien Gang Epidemic: Problems and Solutions," U.S. House on the Judiciary, Subcommittee on Immigration, Border Security, and Claims, Washington, DC, April 13, 2005.

21. This was a salient issue during the official visit of the Central American Presidents to Secretary of Defense Donald Rumsfeld at the Pentagon on May 11, 2005.

22. Richard Tardanico, "From Crisis to Restructuring: Latin American Transformations and Urban Employment in World Perspective," in Richard Tardanico and Rafael Menjivar Larin, eds., *Global Restructuring, Employment, and Social Inequality in Urban Latin America*, Boulder, CO: Lynne Rienner Publishers/North-South Center Press, 1997.

23. *Segundo Informe Sobre Desarrollo Sostenible en Centroamerica y Panamá*, San José, Costa Rica: UNDP, 2002.

24. Jorge Nowalski, *Asimetrías Laborales, Económicas y Sociales en Centroamerica*, San José, Costa Rica: CIDH, 2004.

25. The Inter American Development Bank (IDB) warns that focusing on informal work, however, may be misleading. In admitting that earnings inequality reflects inequality in education, the IDB also claims that education alone is not enough to solve the problem of low wages. See *Inter American Development Bank, Good Jobs Wanted: Labor Markets in Latin America*, Washington, DC: The Johns Hopkins University Press, 2004, pp. 4–5.

26. *Segundo Informe Sobre Desarrollo Sostenible en Centroamerica y Panamá*, San José, Costa Rica: UNDP, 2002.

27. Partnership for Educational Revitalization in the Americas (Task Force on Education Reform in Central America), *Time to Act: A Report Card on Education in Central America and the Dominican Republic*, Washington, DC: The Inter-American Dialogue, 2003.

28. See http://www.mca.gov.

29. United States General Accounting Office, Statement of Frank C. Conahan, Assistant Comptroller General for National Security and International Affairs Before the Subcommittee on Western Hemisphere Affairs, Committee on Foreign Affairs, House of Representatives, March 9, 1989, p. 3.
30. See Sarah J. Mahler, "Constructing International Relations: The Role of Transnational Migrants and Other Non-State Actors," *Identities: Global Studies in Culture and Power*, 7(2):197–232, 2000 and Sarah J. Mahler, "Transnational Relationships: The Struggle To Communicate Across Borders," *Identities: Global Studies in Culture and Power*, 7(4):583–619, 2001.
31. Manuel Orozco, "The Impact of Migration in the Caribbean and Central American Region," *Focal*, March: 2–3 2003.
32. According to Vol. 1 of Hispanic Foods (March 2003), "The growing Hispanic population is exerting a profound cultural effect upon the U.S. as a whole, and consumers from many regions and ethnic backgrounds have developed a craving for 'el sabor Latino'. ... Clearly, the American consumer is 'hot' for the cuisine of Latin America, Mexican of course but with an expanding eye on other Central American nations, as well as opening the palate to the foods of South America and the Caribbean."
33. Sergio de León, "Pollo Campero is Spreading its Wing," *The Miami Herald*, June 3, 2005, p. 2C.s
34. Heather MacDonald, "Immigration and the Alien Gang Epidemic: Problems and Solutions," House Judiciary Subcommittee on Immigration, Border Security, and Claims, April 13, 2005.
35. See "Latin American Regional Report (Caribbean and Central America)," at http://www.latinnews.cp,/lrc/LRC4068.asp, May 29, 2005.
36. Temporary immigration status is for foreign nationals currently residing in the United States whose homeland conditions are recognized by the U.S. government as being temporarily unsafe or overly dangerous to return to (e.g., war, earthquake, flood, drought, or other extraordinary and temporary conditions). TPS does not lead to permanent resident status. As the name indicates, it is temporary, granted anywhere from 6 to 18 months, with extensions.
37. See "Letter to President Bush Requesting Extension of Temporary Protected Status for Salvadorans," *Catholic Charities*, June 30, 2003.
38. Sarah Mahler, "Lives at a Crossroads: Salvadorans in the United States," *Hemisphere*, 8 (Fall):3, 1998.
39. According to Sarah Mahler, op. cit., p. 37, remittances in El Salvador amount to $1200 million a year. Manuel Orozco, "Distant Brothers: The Central American Diaspora," *Hemisphere*, 8 (3) (Fall):32, 1998 provides a much more conservative number but still concludes that remittances are providing more resources than the USAID.
40. Manuel Orozco, "Latino Hometown Associations as Agents of Development in Latin America," Honduras: Inter American Dialogue conference paper, Jan. 31, 2000.
41. Orozco, op. cit. p. 35.
42. Richard Tardanico, "Employment Transformations and Social Inequality: A Comparison of Costa Rica, Guatemala, and the Dominican Republic," *Social and Economic Studies*, 52(3):119–41, 2003.

43. Bulmer-Thomas and Kincaid, *Central America 2020: Towards a New Regional Development Model*, loc. cit.
44. See information at: http://wbln0018.worldbank.org/MesoAm/UmbpubHP. nsf/0/62724610980161ea852569a7001e7896?OpenDocument.
45. Comisión Centroamericana de Ambiente y Desarrollo/UICN, Estado Ambiental de Centroamérica, San Salvador: CCAD, 1998
46. Tim Rogers, "Nicaraguan Legislators Accused of Illegal Logging," *The Miami Herald*, May 30, 2005.
47. Friends of the Earth Fact Sheet, "The Central America Free Trade Agreement (CAFTA) and Environmental Protection," http://www.foe.org/camps/ intl/greentrade/CAFTAEnvironmentFactsheet.pdf
48. See http://proarca.org.
49. Rafael Fernández de Castro, "La Reelección de Bush: Oportunidad Para Reactivar las Relaciones," *Foreign Affairs en Español*, 5(1) (January–March):15, 2005.

Chapter 4

1. There are various names for this free trade agreement, including DR-CAFTA, CAFTA-DR, and simply CAFTA. We will use CAFTA to refer to the agreement.
2. Eighty percent of CAFTA imports already enter the United States duty free under the CBI, Generalized System of Preferences and Most Favored Nation programs.
3. Robert B. Zoellick, "From Crisis to Commerce: CAFTA and Democracy in our Neighborhood," *The Heritage Foundation*, May 16, 2005 http://www. heritage.org/Press/Events/ev051605b.cfm.
4. Henry Nau, "Domestic Trade Politics and the Uruguay Round: An Overview," in *Domestic Trade Politics and the Uruguay Round*, ed. Henry Nau, New York: Columbia University Press, 1989, p. xiii.
5. Thomas M. Franck and Edward Weisband, *Foreign Policy by Congress*, New York: Oxford University Press, 1979, p. 7.
6. Bruce Stokes and Pat Choate, *Democratizing U.S. Trade Policy*, New York: The Council on Foreign Relations, 2001, p. 9.
7. Public Citizen, one of the organizers of the Seattle protests, argues that "over 1000 citizen, labor, consumer, environmental, religious, women's, and development groups from 77 countries have signed on to the new campaign" against the WTO. See "International Seattle Coalition of Civil Society Groups Launch WTO Turnaround Campaign" at http://www.citizen. org/trade/wto/articles.cfm?ID=1582.
8. "The New Trade War," *The Economist*, December 1999; see also "The Lessons of Seattle," *Business Week Online*, December 13, 1999.
9. A useful study that outlined Clinton Administration trade initiatives and their fate in the U.S. Congress is in Robert E. Baldwin and Christopher S. Magee, *Congressional Trade Votes: From NAFTA Approval to Fast-Track Defeat*, Washington, DC: Institute for International Economics, 2000.
10. http://www.whitehouse.gov/news/releases/2002/01/20020116-11.html.
11. Andres Oppenheimer, "Bush's Free Trade Calendar Draws Cheers and Worries," *The Miami Herald*, February 7, 2002.

12. See Central America Department and Office of the Chief Economist Latin America and Caribbean Region, *DR-CAFTA: Challenges and Opportunities for Central America*, Washington, DC: World Bank, 2005, p. 14.

13. The phrase in Spanish, "El CAFTA nos sacará de la pobreza," conveys an even stronger message than its English equivalent. It carries both a fundamental certainty as well as assured hope of things to come.

14. See "Pro-Trade Democrats go AWOL," *New York Times* (Editorial), Jan 13, 2005.

15. Statement, Rep. Charles B. Rangel, Rep. Sander M. Levin, Rep. Xavier Becerra, May 27, 2004.

16. See an undated communication from the Frente Farabundo Martí para la Liberación Nacional at http://www.art-us.org/docs/FMLN0410.pdf.

17. http://www.art-us.org/docs/HonduranDeputies.pdf.

18. Asamblea Legislativa de la República de Costa Rica, May 19, 2004, http://www.art-us.org/docs/CAFTA051904eng.pdf.

19. See the Florida Fair Trade Web site at http://www.flfairtrade.org/index.php?fuseaction=home.Miami.

20. AFL-CIO, Global Fairness 2004, "CAFTA Won't Fix Central America's Deeply Flawed Labor Laws," www.afl.cio/globaleconomy.

21. See http://www.pbs.org/wgbh/commandingheights/shared/minitext/int_loriwallach.html.

22. http://www.citizen.org/about/.

23. http://www.citizen.org/trade/cafta/.

24. Oxfam took a vigorous position against the CAFTA. See "Road Show of Central American presidents can't prevent growing opposition to DR-CAFTA," http://www.oxfam.org/en/news/pressreleases2005/pr050512_cafta.htm

25. See League of United Latin American Citizen, "Press Release: LULAC Opposes CAFTA: Latino Groups Voice Unity against Trade Agreement," July 19, 2004; "LULAC Passes Resolution Opposing CAFTA," *San Antonio Business Journal*, July 16, 2004.

26. See Center for International Environmental Law, "Re: Oppose the Central American Free Trade Agreement (CAFTA)-Recent Released Text Falls Short on Environment," http://www.ciel.org/Tae/CAFTA_18Feb04.html. It is important to note that while many major environmental organizations did oppose CAFTA publicly, others did not, especially those associated with international biodiversity—including Conservation International, the World Wildlife Fund, the Nature Conservancy, and the Wildlife Conservation Society. See Liza Grandia et al., "Are Corporations Hog-Tying Conservation Groups in CAFTA Fight?" *Grist Magazine*, June 2, 2005. http://www.bilaterals.org/article-print.php3?id_article=2014.

27. Not all environmental groups in the region were opposed. Among those supporting the agreement were Costa Rica's Foundation for the Restoration of Nature, Salvanatura from El Salvador, and the Honduran Network of Ecologists for Sustainable Development. See Diego Cevallos, "The Green Promises of CAFTA," http://tierramerica.net/2005/0212/iacentos.shtml.

28. See Federación Costarricense para la Conservación del Ambiente, "Costa Rica Impulsa un Tratado en Perjuicio de los Agricultores, los Consumidores y el Ambiente," *Comunicado de Prensa*, May 2004, http://www.feconcr.org/contents/com-biodiv04.htm.

29. Robert B. Zoellick, "From Crisis to Commonwealth: CAFTA and Democracy in our Neighborhood," *The Heritage Foundation*, May 16, 2005. See "U.S. Diplomacy in Latin America: Hearing before the Subcommittee on the Western Hemisphere of the House International Relations Committee," 109th Congress, 1st Session (2005) (testimony of Jerry Haar).
30. Helio Jaguaribe, "MERCOSUR and the New Global Order," *Hemisphere*, 8(3) (Fall): 24–25, 1998. See also David A. Wernick, "Globalization and Its Impact on Florida's Industry, Workforce and Environment: Public Policy Dimensions," in *Florida's Global Frontiers*. Tampa: University of South Florida Center for Globalization Research, 2005.
31. José Manuel Salazar and Eduardo Spierisen, "Las Economías Pequeñas y de Menor Desarrollo Relativo en el ALCA: Una Posición Centroamericana," in *Política Comercial e Integración Económica en Centroamérica*, San José, Costa Rica: FUNPADEM, 1997.
32. There have been some initiatives that are meant to foster developmental support, particularly the creation of the U.S. Millennium Challenge Account, that are helping El Salvador, Nicaragua, and Honduras for infrastructure and human resources development programs.
33. "CAFTA Win Sends Mixed Signals on U.S. Government—Analysts," *Reuters*, July 28, 2005.

Chapter 5

1. See Gert Rosenthal, "On Poverty and Inequality in Latin America," *Journal of Interamerican Studies and World Affairs*, 38(2/3) (Summer/Fall):15–39, 1996.
2. Saskia Sassen, "Beyond Sovereignty: Immigration Policy Making Today," in Susanne Jonas and Suzanne Dod Thomas, eds. *Immigration: A Civil Rights Issue for the Americas*, Wilmington, DE: Scholarly Resources Inc., 1999, p. 15.
3. Joel Garreau, *The Nine Nations of North America*, New York: Houghton Mifflin, 1981.
4. See Edelberto Torres Rivas, "La Pacificación de la Guerra," *Foreign Affairs en Español*, 1(2) (Summer): 15–19, 2001.
5. Thomas W. Walker and Ariel C. Armony, eds., *Repression, Resistance, and Democratic Transition in Central America*, Wilmington, DE: SR Books 2000.
6. Inter American Development Bank, *Good Jobs Wanted: Labor Markets In Latin America*, Washington, D.C.: The Johns Hopkins University Press, 2004. p 179.
7. See Alexander López et al., *Conflicto y Cooperación Ambiental en Cuencas Internacionales Centroamericanas: Repensando la Soberanía Nacional,* / San José, Costa Rica: FUNPADEM, 2002.
8. The Tuxtla Dialogue bears the name of the capital city of the Mexican State of Chiapas where the dialogue was first held in 1991. This ongoing effort has consolidated a long-standing political and cultural association between Mexico, Central America Belize, and, as of late, Panama, and has facilitated a broad array of trade, security, environmental, and technical cooperation agreements. The importance of this political dialogue notwithstanding, the most significant result of the Tuxtla Dialogue has been the Puebla-Panama Plan, an initiative announced by Mexican President Vicente Fox at his

inauguration in 2000. The PPP, as it is known, constitutes an ambitious—and often severely criticized by Mexican and civil society organizations—mainly infrastructure development proposal (it also includes environmental and social development initiatives) currently coordinated by the Inter American Development Bank. For more information see http://www.iadb.org/ppp/.

9. Kenichi Omae, *El Fin del Estado Nación*, Santiago, Chile: Editorial Andrés Bello, 1997.

10. At about the same time, 11 states in Mexico and the United States formed the Gulf States Accord, a loose coalition of state governments interested in promoting their Gulf of Mexico geographic and economic commonalities.

Index

A

ALIDES, 104
Alliance for Progress, 20, 23–24
Alliance for Sustainable Development, 41–43
American Federation of Labor and Congress of Industrial Organizations, 90
Antiterrorism efforts
    Central American countries participation in, 55–56
    description of, 6
Antitrade activism, 86
Aronson, Bernard, 37
Association of Caribbean States, 106

B

Belize, 8, 10, 41
Biodiversity, 76–77
Bolivia, 78
Brazil, 6
Bush, George H.W., 17, 28, 35
Bush, George W.
    free trade position, 48
    policies by, 47–48
    trade policy, 86

C

Calling cards, 73
Caribbean
    description of, 18
    natural disasters in, 43–47
Caribbean Basin Initiative, 24, 26–27, 36, 88
Castro, Fidel, 20
CBI, See Caribbean Basin Initiative
Central America
    agricultural activities in, 6
    Caribbean and, 106
    communist movements in, 19–20
    democratization in, 4, 61, 64, 100
    diversity of, 7–11
    free trade negotiation with, 86
    future of, 98
    GDP of, 6
    globalization in, 5
    indigenous population of, 8
    international linkages, 26, 39–40, 101
    interpersonal confidence in, 60
    leadership in, 103–104
    leftist political parties in, 19
    map of, 3
    participatory policy-making in, 4
    peace accords in, 37